REVOLUTIONARY CHRISTIAN CITIZENSHIP

"Yoder may have been writing primarily for citizens of a superpower during the Cold War era, but this collection also speaks to Christians in other political contexts several decades later."
—*Paul C. Heidebrecht, Ottawa Office director, Mennonite Central Committee Canada*

"For those committed to taking the words of Jesus seriously and applying them to societal concerns as well as to personal ethics, Yoder speaks with prophetic power."
—*Tony Campolo, professor emeritus, Eastern University*

"This volume is accessible without sacrificing the depth of Yoder's theology—practical without being reduced to pragmatism."
–*Paul Doerksen, assistant professor of theology, Canadian Mennonite University*

"Yoder's influence over the last forty years is substantial. The editors are to be congratulated for extending that witness. Well done!"
—*Mark Thiessen Nation, author of* John Howard Yoder: Mennonite Patience, Evangelical Witness, Catholic Convictions

"This series of volumes should make the thought of our most brilliant Mennonite theologian accessible to a broader audience."
—*Ronald J. Sider, president, Evangelicals for Social Action*

VOLUME 2

Yoder for Everyone

REVOLUTIONARY CHRISTIAN CITIZENSHIP

John Howard Yoder

Edited by John C. Nugent, Branson L. Parler, and Andy Alexis-Baker

Herald Press

Harrisonburg, Virginia
Waterloo, Ontario

Library of Congress Cataloging-in-Publication Data
Yoder, John Howard.
   Revolutionary Christian citizenship / John Howard Yoder; edited by
John C. Nugent, Branson L. Parler, and Andy Alexis-Baker.
   pages cm. — (John Howard Yoder's challenge to the church;
   Volume 2)
   ISBN 978-0-8361-9688-7 (pbk. : alk. paper) 1. Christianity and
politics—History of doctrines. 2. Christianity and politics.
3. Christians—Political activity. 4. Citizenship—Religious aspects—
Christianity. 5. Jesus Christ—Political and social views. I. Title.
   BR115.P7Y65 2013
   261.7—dc23
                                                           2013020193

Note: The new name of the series is *Yoder for Everyone.*

Unless otherwise noted, Scripture text is quoted, with permission, from
the New Revised Standard Version, © 1989, Division of Christian
Education of the National Council of Churches of Christ in the United
States of America.

REVOLUTIONARY CHRISTIAN CITIZENSHIP
Copyright © 2013 by Herald Press, Harrisonburg, Virginia 22802
   Released simultaneously in Canada by Herald Press, Waterloo,
   Ontario N2L 6H7. All rights reserved.
Library of Congress Control Number: 2013020193
International Standard Book Number: 978-0-8361-9688-7
Printed in United States of America
Cover design by Brian Nugent
Design by Merrill Miller/Catie Peterson
Cover photo: composite image by Brian Nugent, including a photo by
   Milos Luzanin/iStockphoto/Thinkstock.

17 16 15 14 13   10 9 8 7 6 5 4 3 2 1

To order or request information, please call 1-800-245-7894 in the
U.S. or 1-800-631-6535 in Canada. Or visit www.heraldpress.com.

Contents

Foreword

How do followers of Jesus relate to the state? Many North American Christians never ask this sort of question. Consequently, they simply assume that their relationship with the state—marked by voting and wearing buttons, or displaying banners and paying taxes—is justified and honorable to God. Since their pastors or favorite writers confirm what they are doing, they are at peace and their postures are justified all over again. It seems that what they are doing is just what the Bible teaches.

Today, however, many Christians are also beginning to wonder. Some even speak up about the glaring contradictions of worshiping the Lamb who was slain by the empire's forces of evil, yet offering themselves without hesitation to the ways of the empires in our world today. Many are wondering about how it is possible to follow the poor Galilean while sitting comfortably in well-furnished homes, entertained by expensive sound systems connected to elegant HDTVs. Many are wondering why the church is so segregated along ethnic, economic, and political lines when the one thing their Savior and Lord prayed for was their unity in spite of race, economic status, or politics.

How then do Christians relate to the state in our day? Here in the United States, they inherit two possibilities. The first comes from John Winthrop, the second from Roger Williams.

John Winthrop is famous for many things, not the least of which is his leadership of the Puritan establishment in Boston, and perhaps even more for his sermon entitled "The Model of Christian Charity." In the sermon, he likens the Puritan experiment at Massachusetts Bay Company to a "city on a hill." That city on a hill became a failed experiment in coercion. As long as one agreed with his or her fellow Puritans—and that agreement had to extend down a long, long list—one was safe. Very few qualified for full membership in the church the Puritans established; some were persecuted, a few were excommunicated, and some put to death.

The Puritan experiment of Winthrop is the Puritan version of Constantinianism. That may sound harsh, especially to one whose faith has many times been nourished by the writings of Puritans (like Winthrop and Jonathan Edwards), but the coercive behaviors of Winthrop's Puritan establishment must own up to their implications. What Nathaniel Hawthorne sketched in graphic and tragic lines in *The Scarlet Letter* or in short stories like "Young Goodman Brown" do not so much distort the Puritan experiment as condemn its realities with bold images and expressions.

There are not many Puritans left in America, though the political Left fearlessly tosses apocalyptic fears into the media as if Puritans are on the verge of reestablishing themselves in the seats of power. Instead, the Puritan experiment has been modified into theories and procedures and strategies that one finds in such thinkers as Abraham Kuyper, who sorted out the relationship of the Christian's relation to the state through the notion of "sphere sovereignty," whereby each sphere (e.g., education, government, art, church, etc.) has its own rules and regulations and ways of procedure. What Kuyper fashioned for Holland in the nineteenth and twentieth centuries takes on new form when it arrives in the United States, but the vision is largely the same: the American Christian thinks it is his or her duty to work hard to build a Christian culture strong enough to influence the wider culture and so bring redemption to various dimensions of American life.

I suspect most American evangelical Christians operate out of this Puritan reshaping and moderating vision of

Kuyper. One sees a kin to this vision in the many works and activities of Carl F. H. Henry, Christianity Today, the Moral Majority, mainline Protestant cultural Christianity, and various forms of liberation theology. To be sure, these are widely different approaches, but the core idea is that the Christian's calling is to influence the state in the direction of a Christian vision. How could they not want what they believe to be good and right?

One of those who suffered at the hands of Winthrop was Roger Williams, who through the powerful influences of leaders in England came to the United States with a singular vision: to maximize individual soul liberty and to minimize the coercive powers of the state. Williams had the courage to run the idea of soul liberty all the way down to the protection of religious pluralism, with a wall of separation between church and state. (By the way, it was Williams, not Thomas Jefferson, who first taught the wall of separation.) Most of America's constitutional leaders, like Thomas Jefferson and Benjamin Franklin, implemented the vision of Roger Williams, though his name rarely emerges in their discussions.

The consequence of these two streams of thought—the Puritan strategy of Christians influencing the state in a Christian direction, and the Williams strategy of a state that works to protect soul liberty—is nothing less than the bed and table and desk and pulpit of American thought and actions. Most people work in the public sector for what they believe to be good and true, and at the same time most also want their individual liberty and conscience to be protected. Whoever gets the most votes is often equated with the way the Christian participates.

These two streams of thought, however, are not the only two even if they are the majority viewpoints of American Christian thinking. John Howard Yoder, known best for his genius work *The Politics of Jesus*, offers a third way—a way that does not seek coercive influence, even if that coercion is by way of the voting majority. Even though the third way rests upon the ideas of Roger Williams, it transcends them. It is the way of ecclesial politics. That is, the church participates in the culture, but its participation is best understood as an alternative politic, one rooted in the life and teachings of Jesus, which emerge from the history of God's ways with Israel.

Yoder's ecclesial politics are rooted, too, in the politics of the cross—a politics of love, service, obedience, and sacrifice instead of violence, abuse, and coercion. His ecclesial politics is a kingdom politics, one that believes the eschatological vision of Jesus is not just for the hereafter but for today. It is to be lived out in fellowship with other followers of Jesus who seek to embody a way of life that reveals to the world the truth of Jesus Christ, our Messiah King. The essays of this book put flesh and blood on the many conversations Yoder had as he worked out a theology uniquely fashioned in an American context—a theology that could not make complete Christian sense as long as it had only the other two options.

—*Scot McKnight*
Professor of New Testament
Northern Seminary

Acknowledgments

This volume has been a team project. In addition to the work of the three editors, special acknowledgment is due Aaron Woods and Jordan Kellicut for transcribing the audio files that were combined to form chapter 1, Elya and Jacob Hess who transcribed chapter 4, Celia Larson who assisted in transcribing several hard copies into editable documents, and Ted Troxell for lending fresh editorial eyes to chapters 1 and 6, which required the most editing.

We are also grateful to Scot McKnight for writing an insightful foreword, the publishing team at Herald Press for moving the document along through production, and Martha Yoder Maust for supporting our efforts to make her father's important work available to a wider audience.

Introduction

"You're interested in politics? That's odd. You didn't even vote for a president last fall." This question, which someone recently asked one of us, represents how many Christians approach faith and politics. They take Western culture's definition of "politics" as a given and then ask who they should vote for and what position Christians should take on hot-button topics like abortion, same-sex marriage, health care, and gun control. They assume that the prevailing political framework—which revolves around terms like *conservative, liberal, Republican, and Democrat*—lays the basic foundation for all discussions of politics. They then bring Christianity to bear on this cultural framework. As a result, believers end up being just as polarized as their culture, with Christians on the political right poised against Christians on the political left.

John Howard Yoder flips this whole framework on its head. Instead of starting with his culture's definition of politics, he begins with the story of Scripture—a story that centers on Jesus and his politics. Rather than assuming an outside definition of all things political, Yoder searches the Scriptures for how divine revelation might frame our thinking. As he does this, it becomes clear that the hard-and-fast line that is commonly drawn between religion and politics is nowhere found in the Bible.

That is because Jesus initiates a very religious and still very political revolution. As Israel's Messiah, he claims the title of king and announces that God's reign is finding its fulfillment in him. He then gathers a community around himself and shows them how to relate properly to God, one another, and wider society in all of its social and political dimensions. But the kingdom that Jesus proclaims is doubly revolutionary. Rather than confront rival kingdoms with violent revolution, he claims that God's kingdom is manifest in service rather than domination, vulnerability rather than coercion, love rather than fear. Jesus teaches his followers how to approach enmity, power, conflict, money, and community in ways that are basic to any genuine political order.

Since the church's core claim—Jesus is Lord—is both religious and political, the life of the church is religious and political. The essays in this volume reflect Yoder's conviction that Christians must corporately live out Christ's lordship in all areas. The first question is not what everyone or anyone should do, but how Christians should order their lives according to God's kingdom, empowered by God's Spirit, and informed by God's Word.

Yet Jesus is not Lord only of the church. He is enthroned over the entire cosmos with all powers and principalities being made subject to him. So Yoder assumes that Christians have something political to say to everyone, including non-Christians and the state. Since all things in heaven and earth—including thrones, dominions, rulers, and powers—have been created through him and for him (Colossians 1:16), the church must bear witness to Christ in all things.

That is what makes our citizenship revolutionary. We are outsiders, "aliens and exiles" (1 Peter 2:11), whose true citizenship is in heaven (Philippians 4:20). Yet we have the nerve to tell insiders how things really are and really ought to be. Unlike most resident aliens, our otherness does not make us indifferent to the kingdoms of this earth. We seek the good of the cities where we live (Jeremiah 29:7) by speaking truthfully about the way human sin infects our life together, our politics. This sometimes puts us at odds with the nations in which we live. But if Christians sometimes come across as being "against the nations," it is ultimately because we are "for the nations"—just as Jesus set himself *against* sin, death, and corruption *for* the ultimate good of sinners. Revolutionary Christian citizenship means continuing the revolution of the servant king who had nowhere to lay his head, but who proclaimed God's reign and its implications everywhere he went.

Yoder for Everyone series

Although Yoder's voice continues to resonate across the landscape of academic Christianity, it seldom falls within earshot of today's average Christian.[1] This is partly because most of his published works were directed toward scholars. Yet on numerous occasions Yoder addressed ordinary Christians in local congregations, college chapels, and spiritual retreat centers. Unfortunately most of this material has not been published or was published in magazines that were not read widely. Some of it has only been available in audio form. The editors of this series have collected, transcribed, and published this material because we believe Yoder's challenge to follow Jesus in all things still needs to be heard outside of academia.

The first volume in this series, *Radical Christian Discipleship,* was published in 2012. It concentrates on how individual Christians are called to follow Jesus completely in every aspect of their lives. It spells out the nature of Christian conformity to Christ and looks at a variety of issues, including finances, time stewardship, self-assertion, nationalism, and truth-telling. Those wishing to take seriously the radical claims of Christ would do well to begin with this volume. For Yoder, "radical" was not a faddish bandwagon to jump on when the time was right. It defined his life and permeated his thought.

This second volume, *Revolutionary Christian Citizenship,* lays the biblical foundation for how Christians might relate to the nations in which they live. Building off of the political nature of Jesus' ministry, it helps Christians think about broad concepts like power, enemy love, and Christian witness to the state. It also delves into specific issues like

---

1. See the introduction in *Radical Christian Discipleship* for more biographical information about Yoder.

voting, taxation, and pacifism. Yoder's most famous book, *The Politics of Jesus*, has often frustrated readers because it enters a long-running scholarly debate midstream. In this volume some of its best insights are finally available in a form fit for most readers.

Volume three, *Real Christian Fellowship*, will be published in 2014. It will focus on how members of Christ's body ought to relate to one another as a community. It deals with core Christian practices including baptism, breaking bread, making decisions, admonishing one another, serving the poor, singing songs, and curtailing practices that deny women full dignity in Christ. This volume is of particular value because Yoder recovers important biblical dimensions of these practices that have been lost over time. Whether one is part of a small rural congregation or a large city church, this collection will breathe fresh air into the everyday life of the body of Christ.

Revolutionary Christian Citizenship

The present volume has three parts. Part one focuses on the witness of Jesus. Because Jesus is not only divine, but also fully human, he furnishes the pattern for our humanity and the standard for our politics. We know God's will for our lives and for all creation by looking at and listening to Jesus. The chapters of this section therefore spell out the political nature of Jesus' ministry, correct common fallacies that cloud people's understanding of Jesus, and beckon us to heed Jesus' invitation to a form of political witness that cannot bypass the cross. The final chapter of this section addresses the important question of how Jesus relates to Old Testament warfare.

Part two focuses on the witness of the church. Not only was Jesus political but he established a new community with a specific political witness. These chapters clarify God's political vision for the Christian community and sketch the basic posture of churches toward the *narrower* political communities that surround us. Since God's kingdom is transnational and truly cosmopolitan, local political entities—whether the city, state, or nation—are more shortsighted and provincial than the global body of Christ. Although some Christians assume that a pacifist like Yoder would have nothing to say to the state, these essays highlight Yoder's belief that Christians, of all people, can and must bear witness to the state. Part three focuses on specific topics of Christian political witness in action. Yoder brings his clear and perceptive analysis to issues like voting, paying taxes, the arms race, and conscientious objection. This section begins with the question most frequently asked of those who advocate a rigorous commitment to enemy love: "What would you do if someone attacked your family or loved ones?" It also includes sermons that Yoder gave on Memorial Day and that helpfully illuminate how Christians might engage national holidays. In sum, part three demonstrates that the biblical and theological perspectives of parts one and two are not pie-in-the-sky ethics. They touch ground on important issues that confront followers of Jesus day in and day out. Combined, these chapters make clear that the Christian peace witness is not grounded in one or two popular proof texts but in a holistic vision of God's work in this world through Christ and his people.

Editorial concerns

Because all of these essays are historically situated, readers should not be surprised to see Yoder engage the Cold War arms race, the USSR, the civil rights movement, the draft question, Vietnam, and other headliners at the time he was writing. Sometimes the editors have furnished a footnote or worked a brief explanation into the text to help situate such references. Readers are encouraged to exercise their imaginations but should have little trouble noting parallels between earlier decades and issues facing the church today. As Christians face the perennial issues that surround citizenship in God's kingdom and residency in particular nations, Yoder's challenge to the church remains relevant today.

Since our goal is to make Yoder's work available in an accessible format, we have edited his writings as necessary to make them easier to read. We have not made changes that would compromise the substance of the original sermons or essays. Sometimes that involved changing word order, condensing an overly wordy sentence, adjusting punctuation, or adding a word or phrase to improve the flow of a sentence. Heavier editing was required for chapters that we transcribed from audio files. We have also conformed Yoder's language to contemporary gender-inclusive standards as was his own practice later in life. Scripture quotations have been converted to the NRSV, except where the original version makes a difference, in which case we identify the other translations in parentheses.

Given the nature of these writings, there were no footnotes in the originals. All footnotes in this book were therefore inserted by the editors. Some clarify situation-specific material that may otherwise be lost upon readers, others indicate where each essay originated, and still others direct readers to resources where Yoder addresses the same topic at greater length. Those wishing to identify additional places where Yoder writes about a specific topic are encouraged to make use of the free online Yoder Index (www.yoderindex.com).

Part One

The Witness of Jesus

1

Jesus and Politics[1]

Christians who care deeply about public witness cannot avoid asking if Jesus was a political person and, if so, what kind of political person he was. This is an important question because most Christian traditions have held that Jesus is not directly connected to what we call politics. This chapter evaluates common objections to the political relevance of Jesus, shows the political significance of Jesus according to Luke's gospel, and discusses what kind of political witness Jesus did and did not advocate.

---

1. This essay combines three lectures. The first, "Was Jesus a Political Person?" was given at Goshen College Chapel, Oct. 22, 1973. The others, "What Kind of Political Person Was Jesus and Why?" parts one and two, were originally delivered at Holden Village in 1978, and are used for this volume with permission. Holden Village is a Lutheran retreat center that frequently attracts high profile speakers. For more information, visit http://www.holdenvillage.org/. Due to the length and informal nature of these lectures, we have had to condense and edit them more than other chapters in this volume. The original MP3s along with a host of others can be downloaded from Holden Village's online audio archive at http://audio.holdenvillage.org/node/3734. For further reading on the topics addressed in part one of this book, see John Howard Yoder, *The Politics of Jesus*, 2nd ed. (Grand Rapids: Eerdmans, 1994).

Objections to a political Jesus

To best understand and evaluate objections to the idea of a politically significant Jesus, we should briefly define "politics." By politics, most people mean the realm of power, wealth, and decision making that makes a wide-scale societal impact. It is more appropriate to say that politics has to do with the *polis*, or city. It is how particular people in a particular place order their lives together. The Bible talks about this from beginning to end. Adam and Eve are given instructions about how they should order the world they live in. Noah, Abraham, Moses, and the prophets are given specific instructions about the shape of human togetherness. Since the Bible clearly addresses political issues, why do some people insist that Jesus is not political?

Divorcing Jesus from politics

I see four reasons why people divorce Jesus from politics. First, people assume that religion is something entirely different from politics. From their perspective, religion deals with the inner side of human existence and politics with the outer. Faith deals with the individual and politics with the corporate. Religion deals with the eternal and politics with the temporal. There are many other ways to slice human existence into spheres that people strive to keep separate from one another. Moreover, many Christians assume that the best way to be Christian is to keep a healthy distance from the nonreligious realms of day-to-day life and history, including politics.

A second reason why people do not see Jesus as political is that he says things that do not appear to "work." Consider money and violence. Jesus says that some people who follow him must give away all their material possessions and that no one should lay up treasures for the future. He also says that people should love not only friendly neighbors but also hostile enemies. I could discuss other examples, like not swearing oaths (Matthew 5:33-37), but these two are probably the most striking. Jesus tells us to do things with money and enemies that do not seem practical from our perspective. We could not run a society that way. If we are honest with ourselves, the real

difficulty here is that we do not want to do what Jesus says
or imitate what he does.

A third reason many assume that Jesus does not apply
to our political experience is the gap between his time and
ours. Jesus lived in a time when many thought that the
world was about to end. If that were the case, we could
afford to live the way Jesus recommends. We could afford
to give our money away because we would no longer need
it. We could afford to love our enemies because soon we
would not have anything to defend or fight against. Since
the world did not end, perhaps the ethics of Jesus does not
really apply to our world.

According to this view, the gap that separates us from
Jesus also has to do with the size of the world he lived in.
Jesus preached mostly in small towns in the countryside. He
addressed a small society and many of the things he teaches
have to do only with individual motivation. He focused on
changing hearts and trusting God. He cared only about how
believers should behave when, for example, someone strikes
them on the cheek or asks for a piece of clothing. Individual
actions and motivations are the focus, so Jesus' model of
human relationships and his sense of right and wrong do
not apply to society or politics. They are thus irrelevant to
anyone with institutional or political responsibility.

A fourth way to divorce Jesus from politics is to assume
that his teachings only apply to some Christians or to some
realms of life. In medieval Catholicism, clergy and monks
were expected to follow Jesus' teaching in the Gospels, but
this did not apply to all Christians. Clergy were uniquely
free from responsibility for war and the police function of
the state. During the Reformation, Martin Luther main-
tained a different sort of division by distinguishing between
law and gospel. In his view, the realm where the gospel
operates is distinct from the realm where law operates. God
rules over these realms in different ways and for different
purposes. Luther's motto was, "You cannot rule the world
with the gospel." Of course we still have to rule the world,
he insisted, so we will have to do so with the law. Jesus is
therefore relevant to personal salvation and forgiveness, but
not to politics.

A few concerns

I have several concerns about how this discussion is typically framed. One has to do with how we think about things to begin with. If we decide that Jesus is not the standard for a given realm of human affairs (in this case politics), then what do we really believe about revelation in Christ? How far will this declaration of independence from Jesus go? How do we decide what other values should guide us and how broadly we should apply them? If Jesus does not guide us in politics because he is on some other level, then what other realms are also free from submission to him?

I am also concerned about this way of framing things because of what Jesus actually taught. Maybe we divorce Jesus and politics because we have been more influenced by our culture than by Jesus. Jesus says to love our enemies, but Western culture says to clobber them when we have to. Jesus says to share our wealth, but Western culture says to get all the wealth we can. Unfortunately, mainstream Christianity has often sided with Western culture and not with Jesus on these matters. In what sense is Jesus our Lord if we give more weight to rival sources of instruction?

In our time we have good reason to be suspicious when Christians take the liberty to run the world in ways that differ from Jesus. After all, running the world by ignoring Jesus has not turned out to be completely successful. We have not solved the world's economic problems by doing it our way rather than his. We have not solved problems of war and violence by handling enemies our way rather than his. For fifteen hundred years we have presumed a mandate to run the world while also presuming that Jesus had nothing to say about the matter. Yet we have clearly not solved the world's problems by placing the way of Jesus on the shelf.

Luke's political Jesus

Having reviewed common reasons why people sometimes separate Jesus from politics, it is necessary to consider some of the biblical reasons why the two belong together. What happens when we examine the Bible with the question of Jesus and politics in mind? Does it verify the common assumption that Jesus is not political? At first I will focus on the gospel of Luke. We will observe a few key points that speak to the issue of whether or not Jesus is politically relevant.

Political expectations

The first chapter of Luke's gospel makes it clear that Jesus came into a cultural setting in which the political agenda mattered to everyone. For the Jews of Jesus' time, political oppression was part of the problem the messiah would be sent to address. The song of Mary in Luke 1 is well known because it has very wide use in our liturgies. But because we are so familiar with it, we may have real difficulty understanding what it meant to its original hearers.

Mary's soul magnifies the Lord. But what is it that the Lord was going to do? "He has shown strength with his arm; he has scattered the proud in the thoughts of their hearts. He has brought down the powerful from their thrones, and lifted up the lowly; he has filled the hungry with good things, and sent the rich away empty" (Luke 1:51-53). This is political and economic language. It is not the language of piety or liturgy; it is the language of radical social change. The powerful get put down, the humble get raised, the rich lose what they once had, and the poor prosper for a change. This is not religious sentiment but radical social critique. When God acts, that is what God is going to do.

At the end of Luke 1 we have another song, this one marking the birth of Jesus' cousin John. His father sings something similar to Mary: "God has remembered his promise that we should be saved from our enemies and from the hand of all who hate us, to grant us that we, being delivered from the hand of our enemies, might serve God without fear."[2] These statements should be taken seriously and literally. The Jews lived under significant political oppression. They had been colonized by the Romans. They had no independence in international relations and they were not a sovereign nation. Heavy taxation made for a life of suffering. Nevertheless, they had hope—but for what? According to Luke 1 their hope was for political, economic liberation. God is going to do this because God made a promise. We hear them saying,

---

2. Yoder is paraphrasing and merging phrases from Luke 1:68-79.

"That promise was made to our fathers and we want that freedom in our own day."

The oppression, however, was not only political and economic; it was also ideological and religious. The Roman oppressors were polytheists and idolaters who ate unclean foods. They violated God's law at the most fundamental points and yet they succeeded militarily and politically. So it was not just a matter of being uncomfortable under oppression—it was a matter of God's honor being challenged. The Jews' concern is not simply a selfish concern for their own welfare. It is a theological concern. They hoped for God to free them because this would prove that God is truly sovereign over world history. It is fair to say that Jesus came into a situation where people clearly expected political and social upheaval. They expected that justice would be done and that God would be honored appropriately.

As we move into Luke 3, we see the beginning of the public movement of John the Baptist. John preaches in the desert that the way of the Lord must be made straight. Mountains will be pulled down and valleys raised in order to make a processional highway for the Lord. John's language provoked questions. The multitudes ask, "What then should we do?" (Luke 3:10). John answers that there is a new economic order coming, that those with two shirts should share with those who have none, and that those with food should do the same.

Two kinds of people are challenged by John and come to him with specific questions about what they should do. It is important to note that they are public people—tax collectors and soldiers—people who represented the order that is going to collapse and be judged. When the tax collectors ask John what to do he tells them to collect only what they have coming. Likewise he tells soldiers not to extort, but to be content with their wages. He asks them to stop using their violent presence as a means of personal advantage. Since both tax collectors and soldiers mostly lived by collecting more than their share, this would be a radical sacrifice.

When Jesus is baptized, a voice from heaven identifies him as the anointed one, the chosen one in whom God has pleasure. Where does this language come from? It is political language. "You are my Son" is found in Psalm 2, which is a messianic enthronement psalm. Enthronement psalms were sung at the coronation of kings in ancient Israel. Jesus is welcomed by the voice from heaven as the one designated to be king. "With you I am well pleased" is found in Isaiah 42:1. It refers to the special servant of God. Once Jesus is designated king, the question arises: How will he go about being a king? The temptation narratives address this question.

Political temptations

The three temptations of Matthew 4 and Luke 4 are much more political than we often assume. Jesus is not tempted over matters of personal holiness; he is tempted as to how to be king. Jesus is in the desert nearing the end of a long fast when the tempter says, "Why don't you make bread?" If this were merely a matter of satisfying his own personal need for nourishment, Jesus would not have needed much bread. People do not break fasts by eating a lot. That Jesus was being tempted to turn a field of boulders into bread (Matthew 4:3) suggests a wider scope. By using his exceptional messianic powers, Jesus could satisfy the people by feeding them. This would be a direct challenge to Rome, which was maintaining political sovereignty by feeding the crowds. In fact, a few chapters later Jesus feeds a large number of people in a desert and they want to make him king. The tempter was right: one way to be king is to feed the masses. This temptation is less a matter of personal ethics and more a question of what kind of king Jesus would be.

Similarly, the matter of throwing himself into the temple courtyard is a temptation about how to be king. This temptation is not simply a random miraculous proof by which Jesus says, "Hey look! I can jump down and not get hurt!" Rather, had Jesus done what the tempter suggests, he would have fulfilled the expectation of Malachi 3:1: "The Lord whom you seek will suddenly come to his temple. The messenger of the covenant in whom you delight—indeed, he is coming, says the Lord of hosts." People do not spend their time watching the temple roof—if Jesus had suddenly appeared in the temple from above, they would have thought he came from heaven. They would assume he had come to take over and clean up the place. That is a very good way to start if you are going to be the messiah. In fact, Jesus does this later on. At the end of his ministry he enters the temple, surprises everyone, and cleans it up. So, again, the question of the temptations is a question of Jesus' self-definition: how does Jesus define his kingship over against the kind of kingship being suggested by the tempter?

Notice that Jesus never says, "No, you got me all wrong. I'm trying to teach you the sacraments. I'm not interested in all this political business; I just want to start a religious institution." He does not tell people that they should not want a king. On the contrary, he claims to be the king they are looking for. Their problem is that they did not know quite what to expect from him. This is why some people are disappointed and reject Jesus. They do not reject him because he was "religious" or "spiritual" rather than political. No, he was political, but in a way they did not like. Jesus did not say, "You are waiting for a king and I'm not going to be a king." He said, "The kind of king you are waiting for is not the kind of king God wants you to have. But God does promise that his kingdom is now breaking into your experience." Jesus' language for that does not revolve around religious ritual or abstract theology. His kingdom language has to do with how to live together, how to make decisions, what to do with power, and what to do about status—in other words, politics.

Political proclamation

The last specific text that I want to look at is Jesus' appearance in his hometown synagogue (Luke 4:16-21), where he reads from Isaiah 61:1-2. The text essentially says, "I am the Messiah. The Spirit of the Lord is upon me because he has anointed me." What is this anointed one going to do? Five things: preach good news to the poor, proclaim release to captives, give recovery of sight to the blind, set free the oppressed, and proclaim the acceptable year of the Lord. We should give this last one special attention. The phrase *acceptable year of the Lord* may not mean much to English-speaking readers, but in the original Hebrew it was a clearly defined term for the year of Jubilee.

In the Old Testament, there is a special time called "the year of the Lord" or "the year of Jubilee." This is described in Deuteronomy 15 and Leviticus 25 where God gives directions for a periodic redistribution of wealth. In ancient Israel, you would get wealthy if you were especially industrious, had healthy children who could help you on the farm, or were a good organizer and had good luck. If you had bad luck, your children all happened to be girls, you got sick, or you were a bad manager, you would generally be poor. The Mosaic Law does not interfere with the mechanism of work and productivity that allows some people to get wealthy and some people to get poor. But the law does state that every fifty years, things will be evened out. Every seven years, there was a year of Sabbath in which the land rested and certain slaves were freed. But in the fiftieth year, the Jubilee year, all land went back to the family who owned it fifty years ago. In this way, the people who had become poor got the chance to start over.

Now we do not know if the Jewish people ever did this. In some ways, the ethics of Moses and Jesus are similar in that we are not sure the world would work if we did it that way. But the message is clear: this land belongs to the Lord. The Lord gave it to us and divided it among the tribes and families, and it should stay that way. You are the stewards. If you do a good job and produce more, more will be entrusted to you. But every fifty years we start over. The grandchildren of the person who lost it get a chance to make good use of their share of God's land. That is the vision of the Old Testament text. Regardless of whether the Hebrews ever practiced it, the prophets expected the messiah to institute it. This is what Jesus reads in Isaiah 61 and then goes on to say, "Today this scripture has been fulfilled in your hearing" (Luke 4:21). In other words, this messianic expectation is coming to pass.

Jesus' political options

In the rest of Luke, the political nature of Jesus is rounded out and confirmed. Most importantly, Jesus creates a new body of disciples. That is a dramatic thing to do if you want to change a society: create a small group of people who are deeply committed to what you are doing and provide infrastructure for living differently from the larger society, rather than just waiting for the whole society to change. To fully appreciate the uniqueness and power of this political option, we need to consider a popular political option that Jesus rejected.

The Zealot option

Jesus launched his political campaign at a time when several rival campaigns were already up and running. Several of these are discussed in chapter 5, but for now it is worth focusing on the political movement that seems closest to that of Jesus. The Zealots were essentially a national liberation front that was advanced by underground rebels who were waiting for the right time to break forth and take over the country. Ever since the Maccabean kingdom faltered in the centuries before Jesus, people zealous for justice (Zealots) had been trying to achieve a righteous revolution. Every decade or two there was an uprising and the Romans always put it down. In AD 66, for instance, the Zealot movement succeeded for a time. They took over Jerusalem for two years—and it took the Romans two more years to defeat the uprising and destroy the city.

The Zealots wanted a righteous revolution. It would be miraculous because God would come to their aid, perhaps by sending angels. It would be righteous because it was for a good cause and against God's enemies. It would be progressive because it would obey the law of God. It would be conservative because it would reestablish the temple and the sovereignty that they remembered from the age of David. The Zealot option always beckons whenever people experience oppression. One can think of numerous examples in today's world where the most obvious response to tyranny or oppression is revolution.

The New Testament alludes to this political reality in various places. One of Jesus' disciples is named Simon the Zealot. Several other disciples may also have come from a Zealot background. This model of righteous revolution was the explicit concern and expectation of a major segment of Jesus' audience. The Zealot path was a real temptation for Jesus. He talked their language, stood against what they were against, and seemed to share their vision for God's intervention to make the world right. Yet ultimately he was not a Zealot—even if this was not always clear to his followers.

The Zealot option was the primary temptation for Jesus. Jesus was not tempted to enter the political establishment and become powerful, nor was he tempted by success in business and the social influence that might bring. Jesus was tempted to righteous revolution. Where do we see that most dramatically? The cleansing of the temple comes close, but Gethsemane is even more striking. We read the Gethsemane story with such piety and reverence that we often do not stop to think what is really going on. Jesus asks that the cup pass from him. In other words, he does not want to go the way of the cross if he does not have to.

What other way was there? The only serious answer is holy war—that is, he would have taken the Zealot option. Zealots believed that when the holy war came God would fight for them, send an army of angels, and secure victory. The holy war would be God's triumph just like in the days of Joshua. Instead of simply letting himself be crucified, Jesus could have fought and defeated his enemies because God was on his side. He reprimands Peter for trying to defend him by noting that he could call twelve legions of angels. A Roman legion was six thousand soldiers, so twelve legions would have amounted to seventy-two thousand angels. This certainly would have given Jesus a good chance of winning the war. According to Matthew, Jesus thought of this as a real option and then set it aside (Matthew 25:52-54)—but he thought of it. And he was put to death because he could be accused of making claims to the throne. When someone was put to death, Roman legislation required a public explanation in order to deter other potential criminals. The public explanation for Jesus' execution identifies him as "King of the Jews." It categorizes Jesus as a Zealot and an insurrectionist.

Jesus' option

Although Jesus was much like the Zealots in his language and in the expectation he came to fulfill, he differed from them in a central way. Jesus did not try to take control of history and manage it from the top down so it would turn out right. This is because Jesus understood that there are two histories represented by two communities. One history belongs to the established community—that is, the world. The other belongs to a specific community with a different history. It is an alternative society that interlocks with the first but is not completely dependent upon it.

Jesus did not invent this view of history; he simply renewed it. Abraham left the center of culture in the Mesopotamian basin to be a nomad. Joseph saved the Egyptian Empire from economic collapse by his wisdom, but he did not merge his people into its culture. Moses took his people out from the dominant society of the time. David set up a kingship and kingdom, but it did not last very long before the kingdom split and the exile happened. The prophet Jeremiah tells us that God gave up on that kind of statehood and that God's people should live in dispersion. The call of Abraham and the call of the prophets was always "Do not be a nation like the others." That is what Jesus renews: he creates a people, a group, a community unlike all others. It differs from the nations in its basic structural characteristics—characteristics that get at the heart of what we call political.

So what kind of political figure was Jesus? He was the creator (or recreator) of an alternative political entity. The word *church* is commonly used today to refer to religious as opposed to political organizations. But the Greek word for church, *ekklesia,* is not a religious word; it is a political word. *Ekklesia* means town hall, gathering, or assembly. It is where people come together to make decisions and to do business. Jesus created a community that conducts its business differently in the following ways:

- Every society has a way of dealing with offenders through some kind of punishment or rehabilitation. Jesus gives people a different way to deal with offenders: to forgive them. He even put this in the model prayer: "Forgive us, as we forgive" (Matthew 6:12; cf. 18:21-35).
- Every political structure has a way of making decisions, such as a monarchy or democracy. Jesus gives his people a way of making decisions through conversation and consensus under the leading of the Holy Spirit (Matthew 18:15-20; Acts 15:22-31).

- Every society has some way of stratifying people. Structures help the political entity stay together. The most obvious examples are the slave or the servant under a master, children under their parents, and women under men. Those were the standard patterns of classification in Roman times, many of which are operative today. By way of contrast, Jesus sets up a society in which equal dignity is affirmed (Mark 9:35-42; Luke 22:25-27).

- Every political entity has some way of dealing with money. Jesus sets up a community that deals with money by sharing it (Mark 10:29-30; Acts 2:42-45; 4:32-34).

- Every political entity does something about tribal identity. That is, it has outsiders and insiders, whether defined by biological, ethnic, or other cultural factors. Jesus creates a community to which everybody belongs, although it will take a generation to make that become clear, as recounted in Acts 15 (Ephesians 2:11-22; Colossians 3:11).

- Every political entity deals with the issue of power in its extreme form of violence and the capacity to kill. Most political units restrict this authority to a few people. In fact, that is one way to define the state: an entity that controls the authorization to kill. Jesus sets up a society in which there is to be no violence (Matthew 5:21-26, 38-48; Romans 12:17-21).

We could look at other examples, but these serve to make the point. Jesus sets up a community that deals with the same issues as other communities, albeit in different ways. This did not liberate Palestine the way the Zealots wanted to, but neither did it destroy Palestine the way the Zealots did once they got control and provoked the Romans into a lethal backlash. Instead, Jesus got a new story going in the world, a new story that was consistent with God's true definition of liberation.

Political, personal, or both?

People sometimes ask, "Can we hold the political Jesus together with the notion of Jesus as a comforting personal savior?" The answer to this question depends on what we mean by a comforting savior. If you find comfort in knowing and doing God's will, then the two are the same. If, on the other hand, your view of "comfort" is your own, and if what you mean by "savior" is a brotherly figure who suits your own tastes, then you are looking for a Christ without a cross. This sort of Christ is not in our Bible and is not God's Word to humanity.

If someone wants Christ without a cross, then they do not want Jesus. Jesus anticipated this. In Luke 14 we have his response to a superficial popularity of the masses, one that probably sent quite a few people away. He says, in essence, "Do not follow me unless you have counted the cost" (vv. 26-35). And he supports that warning with two political jokes. He talks about a king who starts to build a tower and does not have enough money to finish it. Herod had just done that. He talks about a king who started a war and did not have enough troops to finish. Herod had just done that, too. These parables serve as social commentary but also as a warning: "Do not follow me if what you want is a comforting savior."

Does this downplay the element of inwardness and personal authenticity that is so important to modern Westerners? Well, it might, depending on what you mean. If you set the inward and personal over against the outward and political, then you are reading the Bible with modern glasses on. It is a mistake to think, as some Christians have, that you can love your enemies inwardly while you help kill them politically, or that you can love your neighbors inwardly while you patronize or discriminate against them politically. In reality, an apolitical Christianity denies the humanity of Jesus—a denial that the first letter of John calls "antichrist" (1 John 4:2-3). If, on the other hand, you use inward introspection to make your political obedience more authentic, more understandable, more contagious, more sober, and more joyous, then you begin to connect properly the inward and personal with the outward and political.

The politics of Jesus is the meeting point of restored personal authenticity and faithful social commitment. When the God of the Bible comes to humans—whether to Abraham, Moses, Isaiah, Jeremiah, or ultimately in Jesus—he does not come as a mystical guru who instructs us to retreat from the real world. He comes as Messiah, Lord, and Servant: political terms. He calls us to find ourselves by losing ourselves. He enables us to share in his victory as we share in his cross.

2

Jesus and Peace[1]

"His authority shall grow continually, and there shall
be endless peace . . . the zeal of the Lord of hosts will
do this." (Isaiah 9:7)
"Blessed are the peacemakers, for they will be called
children of God." (Matthew 5:9)
"He is our peace . . . he has made both groups into
one." (Ephesians 2:14)
". . . that supplications, prayers, intercessions, and
thanksgivings be made for everyone, for kings and
all who are in high positions, so that we may lead a
quiet and peaceable life in all godliness and dignity."
(1 Timothy 2:1-2)

According to the Bible peace is a promise, a practice, a person,
and a prayer.

What is common to these four passages is that they
avoid a basic assumption shared by most people in our

---

1. This chapter was originally published as ". . . And on Earth
Peace . . ." *Mennonite Life* 20, no. 3 (July 1965): 108-110. For those
interested in further reading on the topics addressed in this chapter,
see John Howard Yoder, *He Came Preaching Peace* (Scottdale, PA:
Herald Press, 2004) and *Nevertheless: The Varieties and Shortcomings
of Religious Pacifism*, 2nd ed. (Scottdale, PA: Herald Press, 1992).

time: that peace can be made. In other words, people typically assume that we can use the power of our minds, our ministries, our muscles, and our missiles to make the world what it ought to be.

The peace that God promises is real, human, social peace. The Bible knows nothing of a "purely spiritual" kingdom. But only God can keep God's promises. The peace for which we pray and even the fragile, partial peace that our rulers sometimes provide is a social reality. Yet the partial "peace" of the Roman Empire, the British Empire, or the various empires of our day has been bought at a price that Christians could not pay. It was purchased by rulers who asked the church for no counsel and whose shrewdest calculations are in the end mocked by history. Nonetheless, human wrath can and will be used to praise God (Psalms 76:10) KJV regardless of what the church does.

Peace is grounded in God

The peace that Jesus lived and that he created by reconciling Jew and Gentile in his people (Ephesians 2:11-15) is fully human, fully social, and no mere state of mind. But that kind of wholeness in loving fellowship can be imposed on no one and certainly not on nations.

According to the Sermon on the Mount, the "doing of peace" that characterizes the children of God is a direction, not an attainment. They do not love because they expect to change the world and make peace, as if their failure to do so would invalidate their strategy. They love because God is like that. They are "perfect"—which, in this context, means undiscriminating in their love—because their heavenly Father is perfect (Matthew 5:43-48).

The label "pacifist" is deceiving if it is understood to mean the ability or even the intention of making the world peaceful. It is the militarists of East and West who promise peace. What sets pacifists apart is not their desire or ability to make peace, but what they do when their neighbors are at war. The point where "pacifist" commitment stands or falls is its insistence on living on the grounds of the peace already made with humanity in Christ—even in a world not yet made whole and regardless of whether or not it "works."

Christian pacifism draws its sustenance from its roots, not from its fruits.

This is not to deny that the witness and life of the Christian community is effective in reconciling enemies and changing social patterns. But this worthy effect is not its guide. Christian obedience is socially effective, but seeking that effect is not an alternative to obedience.

If Christian obedience is radically disconnected from pragmatism, which focuses on effectiveness, and from pharisaism, which justifies itself by its works, then how do we measure and guide Christian obedience? If results do not justify, do intentions or principles? It is perhaps both of these, but it is more. The doing of peace is self-validating. It is its own purpose and reward. Not that the good deed is one thing and the reward another, or the motive this and the measurement that. The doers of peace "will be called children of God" (Matthew 5:9). Yet this title is not a reward distinct from the deed or an effect distinct from the cause. "They shall be called," in the language of Jesus, is no different from "it shall be seen that they are" or even from "they are." Doing peace and being a child of God are the same thing.

Peace is the way to peace

Because peace is a deed to be done and not a state of things to be established, the children of God will avoid justifying means by ends. This way of reasoning asserts that an otherwise evil deed is made good if done on behalf of some worthwhile result. We reject this view in part because the Bible says little about how to make the world turn out right. We reject this view in part because nothing human is justified except by grace and because the character of the means dictates that of the ends. We reject this view in part because in our selfish and finite view of things, our predictions of how our deeds and those of others will end up are usually wrong. But the deeper reason why we may not justify means by ends is that we are not God. To do so would ascribe to ourselves a sovereignty that is not ours and a vision of ultimate purposes that we lack. We can act in ways that reflect and testify to the reconciliation that God has given, but we cannot put the world at peace.

Peace is a people

Because peace is the breaking down of a wall to create one new humanity, Christian obedience will be indifferent to national and ethnic borders and will take delight in overriding them. Christians will refuse to take part in warfare not only because killing is wrong, but because no single land is their homeland and because their unity in new birth with fellow disciples beyond their borders is a higher loyalty than their local ties. The importance of a worldwide Christian peace movement is not that it solves problems theological or political. It cannot. This movement is not valid because it seeks "relevance" by applying pressure or supporting good causes. Nor is its importance validated when it undergirds the vision that the world already has of what "peace" is and how to build it. This kind of alliance with other "forces for good" is its greatest temptation. What is important about the worldwide church is that it is. Its service to world peace is simply to proclaim that fact. Its service to global community is to be a global community and *therefore* to be incapable of blessing war. We should make the common plea read, "Don't just do something, stand there!" The test of faithful Christian witness is its willingness to refuse the short-circuited relevance of local loyalty. Christians should be in each society the advocate of the absent, the spoilsport in every crusade, the living reminder that there is another side of the question. We must be the conscience prodding society's pride, not the chaplain blessing every bandwagon.

Because peace is promised to the world, Christian obedience will not withdraw from centers of conflict. We may not leave the field to those who testify that Mars (the god of war) is Lord after all. God calls us not to withdraw from the social order but to be present in a different way. We should be guided not by avoiding the wrong that others do, but by creatively confounding the powers of this age with foretastes of the age to come. Let them see service that need not be coerced, charity that does not degrade, institutions that do not depersonalize, authority that does not tyrannize, and forgiveness that does not demoralize. Such is the kingdom that is at hand.

3

Jesus and Violence[1]

> "Then Jesus entered the temple and drove out all who
> were selling and buying in the temple, and he over-
> turned the tables of the money changers and the seats
> of those who sold doves. He said to them, "It is written,
> 'My house shall be called a house of prayer'; but you
> are making it a den of robbers." (Matthew 21:12-13)

Just before Jesus took over the temple court, he had entered
the city at the head of a crowd that welcomed him as their
liberator. There would have been a clear connection in people's minds between the triumphal entry and the cleansing of
the temple.

Relatively little attention has been given in Christian
preaching and teaching to the importance of this event, except
to use it negatively. Some people have argued that Jesus' use
of a whip to move the animals is proof that violence is morally acceptable for Christians. In fact, there is no reference

---

1. This chapter was originally published as "Cleansing the
Temple," *Epiphany: A Journal of Faith* and Insight 4 (Spring 1984):
16–18. For those interested in further reading on the topics addressed
in this chapter, see John Howard Yoder, *The War of the Lamb: The
Ethics of Nonviolence and Peacemaking* (Grand Rapids: Brazos,
2009) and *Nonviolence: A Brief History* (Waco, TX: Baylor University
Press, 2010).

to a whip in Matthew, Mark, or Luke. Jesus is described as moving people simply by the authority of his words, using physical force only on the money changers' tables. The whip is mentioned in John 2:13-16, where the account comes at a different place in the story. There it is specifically said that the whip was used to drive out the sheep and oxen. It is intellectual dishonesty to claim that this one event is grounds for justifying violence. Less would this event justify violence against people, much less would it justify lethal violence, and still much less would it justify the institutional violence of war, at least for those who follow Jesus.

Intellectual honesty demands, however, that we recognize that the cleansing of the temple is a dramatic way of demonstrating the claims of God upon the people and city that bear God's name. Jesus does this by means of a disorderly nonviolent demonstration. When we read of sheep and oxen we think of docile animals, but these were young bucks and bulls, physically without blemish, qualified for use in sacrifice.

The meaning of the event

Interpreters differ as to why Jesus condemned what was going on. Was it appropriate to serve the temple clientele by making readily available sacrificial animals and ritually acceptable coinage, but not to make too much money from it? Were the wrong people providing it? Were they providing it in the wrong way? Or did Jesus take these excesses to mean that the sacrificial ritual itself was no longer an apt way to praise God or bring about and celebrate reconciliation? Was it, as one Jewish tradition suggests, that the high priest's family profited unfairly from a commercial monopoly that was enforced on grounds of ritual purity? Is there some special point to Jesus quoting Isaiah 56:7, which refers to the coming of the Gentiles and indicates that the temple should be a house of prayer for all the nations?

Whichever of these meanings was central in Jesus' mind, it is clear that the deed is a messianic symbol. A standard component of the prophetic vision of the coming day of the Lord was that the temple and priesthood would be purged so their sacrifices could be acceptable to the Lord (Malachi

3:3-4). We have no grounds here to distinguish between the temple and its court, between the place of worship and the place of commerce, between the spiritual and the political. The Anointed One comes to set everything straight and he does so with dramatic flair.

In the narrative of Mark it was this offense that moved Jesus' enemies to begin planning to destroy him. John 2:17 records that this event reminded the disciples of Psalm 69:9: "zeal for your house . . . has consumed me." If Jesus' actions can serve as a model for the believer, we need to ask in what sense and for what causes "zeal" is a virtue and whether zealous gestures are desirable. Most occurrences of the Greek term *zelos* are translated as "jealousy." It is often parallel with "strife." Only a few occurrences do not have this more negative sense and translate it more softly as "concern." Even "zeal for God" is of questionable value. None of the Gospel narratives seem to invite the readers, then or now, to place themselves within the story.

The meaning of the event for us

What meaning for the Christian should be drawn from this unique gospel story? Sometimes, perhaps, we participate in the business of ritual religion and turn it into a source of security and advantage. If that is the case, then we may need to see ourselves in the position of the merchants and the moneychangers. Then we face the call to repent and follow Jesus. This call should be heard as liberation, even if the advantage we previously had is taken away.

Maybe, for a few of us, it would be appropriate to think of ourselves as being in the same situation as the "poor of the land" whose access to temple worship was made prohibitively expensive by the priestly establishment. Perhaps we might let our minds play with an allegorical angle that would see our bodies as the "temple," which our jealous Lord wants to see purified of ceremonial paraphernalia so that we might offer the pure sacrifice of our selves, which is our "spiritual worship" (Romans 12:1).

Yet the best way to see ourselves in this story is simply as disciples who recognize in Jesus the kind of human existence that glorifies God and that we are called to follow. For that purpose let us grant that we may sometimes be convinced that we stand in a situation of moral privilege. We think we see injustice and represent justice at some point where the honor of God, the authenticity of genuine worship, and the dignity of the poor are at stake. Seldom is a human being that clearly in the right for that strong a cause. I have never been. I doubt that most of my readers have ever been.

But let us grant that it *could* be the case and that I might represent with overwhelming clarity and righteousness the cause of God's honor and the rights of the exploited. Let it be granted that I would be convinced that I am sent to testify with rare prophetic authority to a point where unworthy motives and corrupt institutions combine to create both social and ceremonial evil. Let it be granted that I am one of the most righteous persons in human experience, facing one of the most evidently corrupt phenomena. It was in the face of such a multidimensional evil and with all the authority of God's special anointing that Jesus proceeded nonviolently to stop Roman soldiers and temple police in their tracks without weapon or force, but with the truth of his personal presence. Even if we were to stretch the meaning of words and make a length of rope into an instrument of "violence," even that "symbolic weapon" would still be closer to being disarmed than to holding a sword or firearm.

The power of Jesus' actions

The more we understand the greatness of Jesus' moral and spiritual power, the clearer it becomes that his action—with no police force, no bodyguards, and no arms—was not only possible but essential to its meaning.

Others had tried to cleanse the temple with force of arms before, but Judaism agreed that the Maccabees had been a failure. To cleanse the temple, city, and land by force was still the Zealots' dream. They seemed to succeed for a time, in the years 66–70 under the leadership of Menachem and again in 132–35 under Simon Bar Kokhba. Yet those efforts were also failures, even militarily. Jesus' temptation in the desert and in the garden of Gethsemane makes clear that what was wrong with the Zealots' mindset was not that it was destined to fail politically and militarily and not that it would lead to martyrdom. It was wrong because it was not the way God's temple or people could be purged. The blood of enemies cannot purify a profaned temple or nation. The sword of revolution or insurrection cannot create a free and just society.

It is fitting that when the Messiah judged those who did wrong, he put his blood at risk, not theirs. We must be willing to do the same whenever we think that we are the bearers of some holy cause.

4

Jesus and Majesty[1]

"Majesty" originally meant being unapproachable. Shortly after
being delivered from slavery in Egypt, the Israelites caught a
glimpse of God's majesty:

> The Lord said to Moses: "Go to the people and con-
> secrate them today and tomorrow. Have them wash
> their clothes and prepare for the third day, because on
> the third day the Lord will come down upon Mount
> Sinai in the sight of all the people. You shall set limits
> for the people all around, saying, 'Be careful not to
> go up the mountain or to touch the edge of it. Any
> who touch the mountain shall be put to death. . . . On
> the morning of the third day there was thunder and
> lightning, as well as a thick cloud on the mountain,
> and a blast of a trumpet so loud that all the people who
> were in the camp trembled. Moses brought the people
> out of the camp to meet God. They took their stand
> at the foot of the mountain. Now Mount Sinai was

---

1. This previously unpublished sermon titled "Witnesses to His
Majesty" was given March 4, 1984, at First Presbyterian Church in
Kalamazoo, Michigan. It is available in handwritten form at John
Howard Yoder Collection, Hist. Mss. 1–48, Box 143, folder "First
Presbyterian Kalamazoo, 1984," Mennonite Church USA Archives,
Goshen, Indiana.

wrapped in smoke, because the Lord had descended upon it in fire; the smoke went up like the smoke of a kiln, while the whole mountain shook violently. As the blast of the trumpet grew louder and louder, Moses would speak and God would answer him in thunder. When the Lord descended upon Mount Sinai, to the top of the mountain, the Lord summoned Moses to the top of the mountain, and Moses went up. (Exodus 19:10-12; 16-20)

Some of that sense of holiness would do us some good. For so long, our civilization has tried to redefine God in terms that could be contained within the dimensions of the human spirit. We need the reminder that there is more. There needed to be divine initiative. This is the God who is identified with storm and battle, the Lord of hosts who moves about in pillars of cloud and fire.

Next, there had to be a mediator. Moses had to be qualified for that task by being specially called. He also needed great courage to walk into that fiery cloud for his people's sake and for God's sake. Although it is crucial, my primary theme is not that we need to deepen our sense that God is holy—so holy that we ought to melt in God's presence. Although it is also important, my main focus is not that we need to renew our sense that it is God's initiative and not ours that provides mediation between creatures and Creator.

We need those themes and that picture in the background if we want to understand the gospel text found in Matthew 17:1-9:

Six days later, Jesus took with him Peter and James and his brother John and led them up a high mountain, by themselves. And he was transfigured before them, and his face shone like the sun, and his clothes became dazzling white. Suddenly there appeared to them Moses and Elijah, talking with him. Then Peter said to Jesus, "Lord, it is good for us to be here; if you wish, I will make three dwellings here, one for you, one for Moses, and one for Elijah." While he was still speaking, suddenly a bright cloud overshadowed them, and from the cloud a voice said, "This is my Son, the Beloved; with him I am well pleased; listen to him!" When the disciples heard this, they fell to the ground and were

overcome by fear. But Jesus came and touched them,
saying, "Get up and do not be afraid." And when they
looked up, they saw no one except Jesus himself alone.

As they were coming down the mountain, Jesus ordered
them, "Tell no one about the vision until after the Son of
Man has been raised from the dead."

We usually call this scene "the transfiguration," putting
the accent on one visual effect, the report that Jesus' face
shone. Often, people simply guess what this is supposed to
mean. We should not have to guess. That detail echoes the
Moses story. At the end of Moses's time on the mountain, we
read in Exodus 34:29-35:

> Moses came down from Mount Sinai. As he came
> down from the mountain with the two tablets of the
> covenant in his hand, Moses did not know that the skin
> of his face shone because he had been talking with God.
> When Aaron and all the Israelites saw Moses, the skin
> of his face was shining, and they were afraid to come
> near him. But Moses called to them; and Aaron and all
> the leaders of the congregation returned to him, and
> Moses spoke with them. Afterward all the Israelites
> came near, and he gave them in commandment all that
> the Lord had spoken with him on Mount Sinai. When
> Moses had finished speaking with them, he put a veil
> on his face; but whenever Moses went in before the
> Lord to speak with him, he would take the veil off,
> until he came out; and when he came out, and told the
> Israelites what he had been commanded, the Israelites
> would see the face of Moses, that the skin of his face
> was shining; and Moses would put the veil on his face
> again, until he went in to speak with him.

The mediator

The person called and enabled to approach God to become
the bearer of God's will becomes, so to speak, transparent
for the glory of God. People can see that Moses's message
and power is not only his own. If we want to understand the
transfiguration we need to see it as the disciples must have, as
a renewal of the Sinai story. Jesus, like Moses, is called and
sent by God. This is the primary contribution of the distant

background to our understanding of this text. Here is the new Moses, the Mediator, the Revealer. Listen to him. But then it matters who exactly this Jesus is to whom and of whom this is said. For that we need to look at the immediate background more closely than we usually do.

Our way of reading biblical texts often cuts them apart. We read just a paragraph of Scripture and then, because it is "Scripture," we try to interpret that paragraph all by itself. But we would not read a letter that way. We would not read a biography that way.

If we look back to Matthew 16:13-28, a kind of turning point in the story, we see Jesus asking, "Who do people think that I am? Who do you think that I am?" Simon Peter said, "You are the Messiah." Jesus responded with two startling statements. First, he said he was going to suffer—not sickness, not inward spiritual suffering—he was going to be rejected and put to death by the leaders of his society. Peter protested, "No! Don't let this happen to you!" Secondly, Jesus had said that his followers too would have to suffer— also not sickness or merely inward spiritual suffering—but rejection by the authorities. He calls it a "cross," and that means the hostile response of authorities to a threat.

So the event we call "transfiguration" did not happen only for its own sake. It is also the answer to the issue and challenge raised by Peter: "I don't want to believe that God's liberator should have to suffer. I don't believe that I should have to suffer as his disciple. I want God's cause to triumph, and me with it." In response to this specific objection, Jesus and the disciples went to a mountaintop to renew the experience of Sinai, to be told that this is the way.

Roads not taken

What else might Jesus have done? What did Peter want? What has this to do with our witness? Our normal way to avoid the cross is to keep away from conflict or to keep away from politics. Jesus could focus his attention on teaching people how to pray and pay their tithes. He could have steered clear of justice questions, like the use of money, materialism, and power. We sometimes call this "quietism." That is our normal preference. It shows every time some religious figure takes sides—whether on the right or the left. Someone will always object, saying, "Politics and religion do not mix." Jesus refused that separation. He went head-on into the agenda of power and justice. His Hebrew name, the same as Moses' successor Joshua, means "liberator." He talked about a kingdom. He told people to handle money differently and to deal differently with slaves, outsiders, and enemies.

What else might Jesus have done? What else did Peter want? What Peter really wanted was a national liberation movement. He wanted might on the side of right. "Right" meant the freedom of Israel, which needed to be won by force of arms and with God's help. He wanted Jesus to be a George Washington or a Fidel Castro.

That was a live option for Jesus more than it would be for us. He lived in a situation where a righteous revolution seemed to be called for. Some of his twelve disciples and many of the multitudes who liked his preaching belonged to the resistance movement which historians call the Zealots. Their cause was righteous. Their enemy was the idolatrous, oppressive Roman Empire. From the desert to the garden of Gethsemane, this was the real temptation for Jesus—not quietism. If he had chosen that way, Jesus would have avoided the cross by winning, ruling, and destroying his and God's enemies.

Yet Jesus did not take that path. He renounced it because he chose to be a servant, not a tyrant. He chose to love his enemies because God does. He chose to be a peacemaker. "Peace" for Jesus did not mean frightening his enemies into submission as it does to some of our politicians. Nor did it mean giving in to injustice. It meant reconciliation *at his expense*. It meant love *for the enemy*. And all of that is what the transfiguration validated in the face of Peter's doubts. All of that—the rejection of quietism and the rejection of violence—is what the heavenly voice thundered: "This is my Son, whom I love; with him I am well pleased. Listen to him" (Matthew 17:5).

Peacemaking with unveiled faces

Many churches and denominations have begun to see with greater clarity the importance of peacemaking. Is this the evidence of a passing phase, a fad to be succeeded in a few years by a new warlikeness? Or is it a real learning in the face of a new situation that will not go away?

The answer to that question may depend on where we begin. Are we simply afraid of war because it threatens us? Are we interested in peace because it would be cheaper and easier? Or does it have something to do with the majesty of the Lord of hosts? Does it have something to do with being under the pressure of an almighty God who has come down to us and gives us no choice? Does it have something to do with a man who in our name mediates for us, who in our name and for our salvation goes up into the fiery cloud and comes back with God's Word—a Word that teaches us to love one another, even our enemies. A Word that teaches us to renounce domination as he did and to be servants instead. A Word that offers us peace not as a program to enforce on others but as a gift, a given, a presupposition.

In one sense *peacemaking* is a misleading term. It gives the wrong picture when it suggests that peace is absent and that we can create it or (even worse) force it on people. Peace has been given to us. Reconciliation has been accomplished for us and we are to act it out. We do not make friends of our enemies. God has done that. We are called to accept this new reality and to act on it. The old proverb is right: "There is no way to peace. Peace is the way." If we do not decide now to love our enemies, our unloving behavior will never bring us to a place where we can.

We too go up into a fiery cloud and become mediators, transparent to the glow. We will not do that in our own strength. In our own wisdom we will not see how to. But if we serve the Lord of hosts, the Holy One of Israel—who called Moses, Elijah, and Jesus up the mountain to teach us his ways—if we come to God in reverence and trust as Peter did the voice that said, "This is my Son who pleases me...hear him," then it may give our life direction as it did for Peter. That may very well jeopardize our national interest—as some define it—but if so, it would be for the sake of a far better vision of national community. It may well cost us something to steer a path between quietism and violence. It cost Jesus his life. But if the God we serve is the one who accredited Jesus—and if the Jesus he sent is the one in the Gospel accounts—then we do not have much choice. To be doers of peace is not optional if we are God's children.

5

Jesus and Old Testament Warfare[1]

Many Christians commit to nonviolence because of their commitment to Jesus. Such Christians cannot avoid a basic question of interpretation: What do you do about the Old Testament? When modern readers explore the Old Testament, it stands out that violence is not merely tolerated but promoted and glorified. We see this especially in (a) the holy warfare in the time of Moses, Joshua, and the judges; (b) the civil laws of Torah with their insistence upon the death penalty and other kinds of retaliation that breathe a spirit other than forgiveness; (c) the importance of the national existence of

---

1. Originally published as "If Abraham Is Our Father," in *The Original Revolution: Essays on Christian Pacifism* (Scottdale, PA: Herald Press, 1971). This original piece was quite technical at points, so the editors have worked to simplify it wherever possible. Those who wish to make academic use of this article are encouraged to consult the original. Anyone interested in reading further about Yoder's perspective on this topic are encouraged to read Yoder's "From the Wars of Joshua to Jewish Pacifism," in *The War of the Lamb: The Ethics of Nonviolence and Peacemaking* (Grand Rapids: Brazos, 2009) and John C. Nugent's *The Politics of Yahweh: John Howard Yoder, the Old Testament, and the People of God* (Eugene, OR: Cascade, 2011).

the kingdoms of Israel and Judah with its emphasis on the fate and fortune of the kingly house; and (d) the places where psalmists and the prophets rejoice at the potential destruction of Israel's enemies.

In response to the violence of the Old Testament, there seems to be only a limited number of possible explanations. Here I discuss four that recur throughout the centuries.

A new era

In the Sermon on the Mount, Jesus says six times, "You have heard it said . . . but I tell you . . . " Many interpret this to mean that Jesus is announcing the beginning of a new era in world history that simply sets aside what came before. According to this view, we should not be embarrassed about any contradictions between the Old and New Testaments. Jesus declared that some things from the Old Testament are no longer relevant. He introduced a new covenant with new rules. Problem solved.

This approach appeals to those with a progressive or evolutionary view of religious truth. It also fits with a certain view of divine sovereignty. God can change the order of things whenever God wants. That is what it means for God to be in charge. God is not accountable to anyone for any apparent inconsistency or contradiction. The conservative position known as "dispensationalism" sees as many as seven different eras (or dispensations) during which God relates to humans in different ways. The movement from one era to the next is the forward movement of history. Since God purposefully makes each move, we should not view any of them as a contradiction.

This position attracts many serious thinkers, but it has two serious shortcomings. First, Jesus does not say he is setting aside the Old Testament. When he says, "You have heard it said . . . ," he does not go on to quote the Old Testament. Instead, he quotes bad interpretations or abuses of Old Testament laws. Rather than finding fault with the Old Testament, Jesus clarifies its original intent. Before he gives his own commands ("But I tell you . . ."), he says that he demands a righteousness greater than that of the scribes and Pharisees (Matthew 5:20). Instead of abolishing the law, Jesus says that he is going to fulfill even the smallest letter of the law (Matthew 5:17-19). If we pay attention to the context of the Sermon on the Mount, we can see that Jesus has no intention of setting aside the Old Testament law.

A second shortcoming is that if we are talking about the abolition of a legal code, we need to be clear about exactly when the old has been abolished and by whose authority. Is the whole Old Testament done away with or just a particular legal requirement? If only a few segments are done away with, then how can we figure out what is still valid? Does Jesus, a devout Jew, really intend that nothing would be left of the authority of his people's Bible? If everything is not abolished, then we need a careful procedure for determining what is abolished. This type of procedure is not self-evident. It is one thing to say that God is in control and has the right to make and change laws. But it is another thing for humans to attribute a change of purposes to God when God has not clearly said so.

Jesus claims to be the fulfillment of Israelite faith and Jewish hope. The God of the Bible claims to be a faithful and reliable witness. Both of these claims are seriously jeopardized by the idea of a sweeping shift of eras. This is especially so if we lack a clear understanding of the exact nature of the shift, why it happened, and how far it goes. The words of Jesus in Matthew 5 do not sweep away our problem. If they did, they would sweep away the entire Old Testament, which is clearly not their intent.

A concession to disobedience

There may be another way to interpret Jesus' words, "But I tell you . . ." These words could point to a new stage in defining and bringing God's purposes to pass. We could say that God's purposes have always been the same, but that God made a concession because in Old Testament times disobedient humans were not willing or ready to accept and obey God's fullest intentions. There is a shift from old to new, but that shift comes because God ends the concession.

The strongest support for this approach is the way Jesus interprets Deuteronomy 24 on the topic of divorce. "It was because you were so hard-hearted," Jesus says, "that Moses allowed you to divorce your wives, but from the beginning it was not so" (Matthew 19:8). Now that Jesus has restored our knowledge of God's original purposes and our ability to obey, the concession to Israel's hard hearts and closed minds is withdrawn.

This position has several logical advantages over the previous one. It recognizes a real shift in God's commands, but it gives a more thorough account of this shift. It does not simply point to God's arbitrary will or unknowable purposes. Humanity, not God, is responsible for the concession. God's response was rooted in patience. It was never really God's ultimate will.

This approach also has shortcomings. How do we get from the logic of divorce and marriage to the question of violence and nonresistance? Do war and divorce have common links in the Old Testament that would encourage us to make the same move? Do nonresistant love and marriage have any common link in the New Testament? Perhaps there is some kind of parallel, but God's concession is made abundantly clear with regard to divorce and not war.

In addition, this approach does not quite fit the shape of the Old Testament material. Divorce is never commanded in the Old Testament. It is only grudgingly permitted in a context where the main intent is to limit divorce and protect the dignity of women. The same could not be said about holy war or the death penalty. For these issues, the concept of a concession is completely foreign.

An educational strategy

Perhaps instead of adjusting to hardness of heart, God was adjusting to primitive moral immaturity. Insight into the destructive effects of violence and the redemptive effects of love can be attained by cultures only after they advance through several stages. God's ultimate values would have been too much to ask for the rough and illiterate people of Moses's day. By the time of Jesus, however, the Israelites had learned numerous lessons from the prophets, the experience of exile, and Roman rule. So Jesus' call to suffering love was much more realistic in the first century.

This educational approach can be compared to the familiar task of parenting. At the age of two, a parent would command a child not to touch matches or electrical outlets. A few years later, a parent might instruct the child in the proper use of matches and electrical outlets. The parent is not being inconsistent. The nature of fire or electricity has not changed. But there have been changes in the ability of the child to understand and use them. Parents may permit certain actions that they had previously prohibited because the child now understands how to do them properly.

One difficulty with this position is that it views human society in evolutionary terms. It looks down on the ancient Israelites with a sense of moral superiority that is difficult to justify. One must also take a rather loose attitude toward the authority of Scripture. In the Bible, God gives specific instructions that do not easily fit under the heading of "adjustment to immaturity." In the Bible, the analogy of the child's use of fire is significantly reversed. In the case of Israelite warfare, the command to use dangerous weapons comes early and the prohibition comes late.

A distinction between realms

The three previous views all interpret Old Testament warfare as less favorable than New Testament nonresistance. They all have significant shortcomings. In light of those shortcomings, mainstream Christian thinkers have resolved the problem by dividing the biblical materials into different levels or realms. They reconcile the Old and New Testaments by arguing that they are simply talking about different subjects. The Old Testament provides ethical instruction for the civil order and the New Testament provides instruction for the individual. With this approach, one can see the Bible as a total unity. All of its truths and instructions are timelessly valid and without contradiction. All we have to do is recognize a distinction between different subject matters.

The Old Testament narrative deals with the civil life of the Hebrew people. God gave commands and permissions that enabled the civil order to defend itself. This included the use of violence against outside enemies and inside threats to society. These commands, according to this view, give legitimacy to the death penalty and military violence in their time and ours. The New Testament does not deny or retract any of this. It cannot do so because it is not talking about the same subject. Nothing in the New Testament sets standards for the civil order. The only New Testament texts that speak to that issue are those that recognize the civil order as being the master of its own house. It makes statements like "Give to Caesar what is Caesar's" (Matthew 22:21 NIV) and "Be subject to the governing authorities" (Romans 13:1). The ethic of the New Testament, which speaks of nonviolence, the renunciation of rights, and the willingness to suffer, is only for individual Christians to apply in their personal relationships or in the church. Thus there is no contradiction.

This approach has the great advantage of not really needing to solve the problem. It simply denies that there is a problem. Yet it, too, has significant shortcomings. They surface when we attempt to draw a neat line between the individual and the social. They also surface when we recognize that the New Testament says far more about social and political order than simply to obey Caesar. There is a further flaw when one asks exactly what in the civil laws of the Old Testament provides guidance for the modern civil order. Does this include specific details about massacring a city in a holy war or stoning young people who talk back to their parents? Or is it only the general principle of civil order? If so, how do we draw the line between general principles and specific applications? Another weakness of this approach is that it does not recognize any movement in the course of redemptive history. Yet redemptive history is a matter of promise and fulfillment or prediction and expectation. This assumes some kind of change.

A contextual view

Most of the above approaches state the problem by looking back upon the Old Testament from the New Testament. In other words, they assume that God is always the same and is most clearly revealed in Jesus. They then ask: How could God consistently command something different from Jesus at an earlier time? When we look at the Old Testament from the perspective of the New Testament we are struck by the difference between them. This difference seems to lie at the point of whether killing is forbidden or not. But the story is not told that way. It does not reflect back on the Old Testament from the perspective of the New Testament. On the contrary, it recounts a purposeful movement in the opposite direction.

When we look at the events of the Old Testament as they happened and then look forward to the New Testament, things appear quite different. When we read the Old Testament story, we should not first ask how it is different from what came later. Instead, we should ask how it differs from what went before it or what was common at the time. We can then ask whether and how it moves toward what comes later. If we put the question this way, we find that the diversity of commands regarding killing is not the basic issue. The basic issue is an understanding of the covenant community and its relationship to the God who called it into existence and promised to care for it.

This need to focus on the meaning of the Old Testament in its historical context can be illustrated by looking at God's command that Abraham sacrifice his son Isaac (Genesis 22). This passage is itself consistently misinterpreted when we interpret it from the present rather than its original context. We know that a man killing his son, especially in a bloody ritual, is morally and culturally abhorrent. As we interpret the story, we question how a man can deal with a divine command to do something that is abhorrent. We wonder what it says about divine sovereignty since God reserves the right to command us to do such terrible things.

But in Abraham's culture, as odd as it may seem to us, there was nothing morally or culturally abhorrent about sacrificing one's firstborn child. Abraham's neighbors did the same thing. It was natural to sacrifice one's firstborn son. God (or the gods) were deemed responsible for the fertility of one's wife and this sacrifice was a way of assuring her future fertility. The Israelites and their neighbors followed a similar logic when they sacrificed the firstfruits of their flocks and fields. Fertility is a divine gift, so the firstfruits of the womb, flock, and fig tree belong to God. We misunderstand the Abraham story entirely if we interpret it as the paradoxical command of God telling a human to do something awful.[2]

Another modern misunderstanding is our focus on the emotional attachment of a man to his child. Our culture emphasizes a deep sentimental attachment of fathers to sons. For a modern father to take the life of his son is unthinkable. So we wonder what this passage tells us about divine sovereignty or God's character that God would ask a man to do something so contrary to his deepest nature and drives. But again we modernize. This kind of sentimental attachment between father and son was not the same in Abraham's day as in ours.

What then was the test put to Abraham? The wider story of Genesis (and Hebrews 11) makes clear that the test was whether Abraham would trust God for his survival. Isaac was his only legitimate son, and God had promised that Abraham would have numerous descendants. How could Abraham have descendants if his son was dead? It was the promises and purposes of God that were at stake, not just the personal interests of Abraham. The question was not, "Can I sacrifice my interest to God?" but "Can I obey God when doing so seems to jeopardize God's own purposes?" The answer, "God will provide," is not primarily about our own survival or comfort. Rather, "God will provide" affirms that it is rational to obey God even when doing so seems to jeopardize God's own purposes.

Application to Old Testament warfare

This exercise in questioning our cultural assumptions prepares us to interpret the phenomenon of holy war in ancient Israel. Here we may follow broadly the pioneering study of Gerhard von Rad and Millard Lind.[3]

---

2. In the original, Yoder refers to Soren Kierkegaard and Dietrich Bonhoeffer as examples of those who emphasize this type of point because they focus on the text through the lens of modern points of view.
3. Gerhard von Rad, *Holy War in Ancient Israel*, trans. Marva J. Dawn and John Howard Yoder (Grand Rapids: Eerdmans, 1991), and Millard Lind, *Yahweh is a Warrior* (Scottdale, PA: Herald Press, 1980).

What kind of social phenomenon was holy war in ancient Israel? We should ask not how it differed from New Testament discipleship, but how it was original in its own cultural context.

To understand the phenomenon of holy war, we can apply five principles that we learned by interpreting the Abraham story in its context.

1. Do not make hasty interpretations that come from trying to apply the very same command to ourselves before doing any other interpretive work.
2. Interpret the positive meaning of the text in terms of the cultural options of its own time and place.
3. Identify the element in Abraham's decision that is translatable to other situations.
4. Take our cue from the New Testament use of the same account (Hebrews 11).
5. Interpreting the material this way, we have found that whether killing is right or wrong is not the right issue to begin with, at least if we want our interpretation to be fair to the kind of story we are reading.

With this in mind, let us return to the religious warfare of the early Old Testament story. Certain elements are present throughout the narrative from the Red Sea to King Saul. For starters, the issue of whether it is right or wrong to take life does not arise in these accounts. None of these texts relate holy war to the command "You shall not murder" (Exodus 20:13). The Old Testament does not argue (like just war theory) that killing is wrong except in certain circumstances. At this point, nobody thought the prohibition of killing in the Ten Commandments had to do with wars.

The holy war of ancient Israel is a religious event. It is depicted as a ritual. The accounts of holy war give a prominent place to the term *herem*, which means "set apart" or "taboo." Before being attacked, a Canaanite city would be "devoted to Yahweh." This was a ceremony that made the entire city, including its inhabitants, a sacrificial object.

The bloodshed was not viewed as the taking of the lives of individual persons, each of whom could be thought of as a father or a mother or a child. Instead, holy war was a massive, bloody sacrifice to the God who had given the enemy into their hands. Enemies are put to death not because Israel hates them on a personal level but because, in a much more ritual way, they become a human sacrifice.[4]

This ritual context has an economic side effect. If all the slaves and flocks of the enemy are slaughtered in one vast sacrifice, there will be no spoils of war. The war does not become a source of immediate enrichment through plunder. Nor is it a source of squabbling among soldiers over how to divide the spoils; there are no spoils.

Old Testament holy war is not the predictable result of strategic planning but an ad hoc charismatic event. Israel falls under the pressure of neighboring enemies and then a leader arises who is not a part of any royal dynasty or professional military class. In response to the leader's call, the men of Israel arrive with their own weapons, typically whatever tools they had just been using (axes, hoes, etc.). There is no professional army or military strategist. If Israel's forces win, it is not because they had greater expertise or numbers. It was a miracle: "the Lord had given all their enemies into their hands" (Joshua 21:44). Sometimes, as in the parade around Jericho and the wars of Gideon, special symbolic measures are taken to make clear the nonrational, nonprofessional, miraculous character of the entire battle. When the Israelites want to have a king and standing army like other nations, however, the miraculous holy wars come to an end.

What, then, did the original experience of holy wars mean for Israel? The key point is that their survival was entrusted to the care of Yahweh, their king. They did not need to trust

---

4. Before we judge this perspective as being barbaric, we ought to think about whether contemporary warfare views enemy soldiers in a significantly different light. Enemies are not viewed as children, spouses, or siblings, but as "collateral damage" or lives to be sacrificed in light of the greater cause of one's nation. We even honor those who fight for our country for "sacrificing" their lives on our behalf. The Old Testament is simply more transparent in acknowledging that the Israelites were also sacrificing the lives of their enemies [Editors' note].

their own institutional readiness or the stability of their royal house. Yahweh would provide.

This interpretation of the central meaning of holy war is supported by the later prophets and the writer of 1–2 Chronicles. They do not conclude that because Israel slaughtered the Amalekites they should put to death all of God's enemies. Rather, they believed that because Yahweh had always taken care of them in the past, they should trust God to provide for their immediate future. The holy war tradition, as interpreted by later generations, worked against the development of a military caste, military alliances, and political strategy based on military power.

There is another element as well. According to von Rad, the picture given by a superficial reading of Joshua is misleading. It gives the impression of a rapid military sweep across Palestine within a very limited period. These military operations appear aggressive and strategic. According to critical historical reconstruction, however, it seems more likely that the Israelites gradually infiltrated the spaces between the Canaanite settlements and eventually became more settled and less nomadic. As they settled in, they were threatened by the earlier inhabitants of the land and had to deal with them somehow.

So as we read the book of Joshua we must also pay attention to other biblical reports of Canaanite cities that continued in the midst of Israel for generations. Within the same territory, there are Philistines, Canaanites, Ammonites, and other very close neighbors. Although the infiltration of the Israelites into Palestine was aggressive to some extent, the actual holy war military operations tended to be defensive.

The case for the historical view

When we focus on the meaning of Old Testament warfare in historical context, we avoid being condescending and arbitrary toward the ancient Hebrews. We avoid saying that they mistakenly thought that God told them to fight or that God made a "concession" in response to their conscious disobedience. We can affirm that in these events there was, as the story says, a real word from Yahweh of hosts (armies), who spoke to Israel in historically relevant terms.

The experience of holy war speaks to a particular issue: the readiness of God's people to depend upon divine miracles for survival. The holy war of Israel is the concrete experience of not needing any other crutches for one's identity and community than trust in Yahweh. Furthermore, because Yahweh is king, it is not necessary to have earthly kings as do the neighboring nations.

From the ancient Hebrews through the latter prophets and up to Jesus there was real historical movement, real "progress." But the focus of this progress was not a changed ethical code but an increasingly precise definition of what it means to be God's people. The identification of the people of Israel with the state of Israel was progressively loosened by the events and prophecies of the Old Testament. It was loosened by the development of a growing vision of Yahweh's concern for all people and by the promise of a time when all people would come to Jerusalem to learn the law. It was also loosened by the development of a concept of a faithful remnant, which no longer assumes that all Israel as a geographical and ethnic body would be usable for Yahweh's purposes.

These two changes altered the relevance of the prohibition of killing. Once all people are seen as potential partakers of the covenant, then the outsider can no longer be perceived as less than human or as an object to be sacrificed. Once one's own national existence is no longer seen as a guarantee of Yahweh's favor, then one no longer expects miracles like holy war to save one's national existence. Thus the concept of holy war is not dismantled by the declaration of a new ethical demand, but by a restructuring of the Israelite perception of community under God.

Of the other viewpoints sketched earlier, the "educational strategy" is the most usable. This view sees God as teaching humans certain things as they are ready through the process of redemptive history. This view is problematic, however, if we see it as focusing on ourselves, the hearers, rather than on the God-driven course of events. The education motif gives us the picture of a curriculum through which all pupils can move at their own speed. But a learner-centered picture is deceptive. Salvation history has a firmness and finality to it that does not fit with the picture of a repeatable curriculum. Jesus came only once in the fullness of time because his hour had come. He did not come because a certain number of Jews reached a point in their syllabus where they were ready for what God was going to teach next. The real working of a real God in real history cannot be reduced to progressing through a curriculum at a certain rate determined by the capacity of the learner. Furthermore, it may not be accurate to say that people are any more "ready" or "mature" today than in Jesus' time, nor in Jesus' time than in Joshua's.

We should not draw a sharp line between an Old Testament that permits killing and a New Testament that does not. Instead, we will observe positive movement along coherent lines, beginning with what is new in holy war and moving in continuous steps to what is new about the man Jesus. Already in the very first steps of the Old Testament, the theme of dependence upon God for one's existence is new. Already in the earliest legislation of Israel there are novelties, such as the rejection of indirect retaliation, which was part of the laws of other ancient peoples, and greater dignity given to women and slaves. The prophets progressively underline these same dimensions as the story continues. This movement continued in a variety of ways: non-Israelites were incorporated into the tribe, the vision of Israel's calling expanded to include other nations, the prophets criticized the way the Israelites saw kingship and territorial sovereignty as central to their identity, and history ultimately confirmed the prophets' criticism in that kingship and territorial sovereignty fell by the wayside.

This movement ultimately culminated at the point where John the Baptist opened the door for Jesus: "Do not begin to say to yourselves, 'We have Abraham as our ancestor'; for I tell you, God is able from these stones to raise up children to Abraham" (Luke 3:8). To be the children of Abraham means to share the faith of Abraham. Thus the diminishing significance of ethnic-political peoplehood is completed in both directions. There is no one in any nation who is not a potential child of Abraham, since that family relationship is a miraculous gift that God can open up to Gentiles. On the other hand, there is no given ethnic-political peoplehood that can defend itself against others as bearer of the Abrahamic covenant, since those who were born into that covenant can and did jeopardize their claim to it by their unbelief. The willingness to trust God for the security and identity of one's people was the original concrete moral meaning of holy war. That original willingness is now translated into the willingness to renounce the earlier definitions of one's people and of one's enemies that gave holy war its original meaning.

Part Two

The Witness of the Church

6

God's People and World History[1]

When we think about the social realm, we often focus on two centers of attention. One is the individual. The individual is the one who has faith, who may be alienated from God, or who may be saved. The individual is also the one who makes decisions, so it is fitting to talk about his or her motivation, guilt, or repentance. The other focal point is history as a whole. When we think of history, we usually focus on nations and the governments that speak for them. Sometimes we think of other global entities, like civilization or the economy, but we tend to think of history as the broad scope of events that make up the big picture.

Most discussions of Christian social ethics revolve around the relationship between the individual and these large social

---

1. This chapter was originally a 1978 lecture at Holden Village entitled "Alternative Community and Social Ethics." As with chapter 1, due to the length and informal nature of this lecture, we have had to condense and edit this material more than other chapters in this book. For those interested in further reading on the topics addressed in this chapter, see John Howard Yoder, *The Priestly Kingdom: Social Ethics as Gospel* (Notre Dame: University of Notre Dame Press, 1984) and *The Royal Priesthood: Essays Ecclesiological and Ecumenical* (Grand Rapids: Eerdmans, 1994).

structures. Christians do not necessarily agree about how these two are interrelated and whether one is more important than the other. Such discussions are important, but we need to be aware that, biblically speaking, this is not the whole picture. In the biblical vision, there is not simply the vast stream of history on the one hand and the individual on the other. There is a third element: a distinctive community that is not simply a group of individuals. It is a distinctive elect, a specific group called out from the wider society. The founder and symbol of this group is Abraham, who is told that through him all nations of the world will be blessed. But the way from Abraham to the blessing of all the nations is a distinctive people. The identity of that people is a central theme of Scripture.

Discovering our place in world history

There is a strange story in Numbers 22–24. As Moses and his people are making their way to the Promised Land, one of their enemies, King Balak, seeks someone to prophesy against these intruders. So he summons Balaam who goes to a mountain to prophesy. Unfortunately for Balak, the oracle comes out *for* the Israelites instead of against them. But what is the picture Balaam sees when he gets on top of that mountain? "For from the top of the crags I see him, from the hills I behold him. Here is a people living alone, and not reckoning itself among the nations!" (Numbers 23:9). This is a description of the distinctiveness of the people of Abraham and Moses. They are different because they do not consider themselves a nation like the other nations.

One of the technical terms for this idea is "priestly kingdom," which we find in Exodus 19. Just before giving the Ten Commandments, God says to the people through Moses, "You have seen what I did to the Egyptians, and how I bore you on eagles' wings and brought you to myself. Now therefore, if you obey my voice and keep my covenant, you shall be my treasured possession out of all the peoples. Indeed, the whole earth is mine, but you shall be for me a priestly kingdom and a holy nation" (Exodus 19:4-6). The apostle Peter alludes to this passage in 1 Peter 2:9, giving us four phrases, each of which describes the same communal reality:

chosen race, royal priesthood, holy nation, and God's own people. Each has a noun modified by an adjective describing the community's distinctiveness. The idea of being a priestly community surfaces again in Revelation 5.

We need to grasp the significance of this observation. In God's purposes, the reality of the people of God stands between the course of global history and the life of the individual believer. This fact is lost when we define the big picture of world history in ways that are narrower than God's world. When we talk about the meaning of history, we usually mean the fate of Western civilization, which is centered in North America, which is centered in Washington, D.C., which is centered in the White House. Yet every one of those centerings is false. What we really play over against the church is not the big picture of God's world, but some other finite group, some other provincialism, nationalism, ethnic identity, or privileged group.

Let us return to the biblical material. The value of an alternative community begins with the biblical message that God has chosen to work through such a community. He told Abraham to be an alternative to Chaldea. Chaldean kingship was an enormously powerful social and religious event. Chaldean culture linked religion, science, and social organization in such a way that they were able to irrigate the valleys of Mesopotamia with skills and means that have been lost for thousands of years. Chaldea was a highly organized society and Abraham was called to leave it completely.

Abraham leaves it all behind to begin a different kind of history. He gets to the land that is supposed to be his, but he is not able to possess it and soon has to leave it. After a while he returns, stays there a couple generations, and his children have to leave again until Joshua eventually brings them back. When they are finally situated in the land, we see a tug-of-war between God's intentions for them as a covenant people and Canaanite models of kingship and community that were very different. Some people want kings like the Canaanites. Samuel and Jotham say, "That's not what we need. God is our king." But finally the people want it so much that God gives in and Samuel lets them have a king.

They spend the next several centuries on a failed experiment with Canaanite kingship. Remember, David's soldiers were not Hebrews because sons of Abraham did not have the skills of soldiering. So who was the man whom David had killed in order to take his wife? Uriah *the Hittite*. The Israelites recruited foreigners to serve as generals because they did not know how to run an army themselves. The statecraft that it took to set up the Davidic kingdom was borrowed from the Canaanites, and Samuel knew it. Jotham's fable in Judges 9 is a biting sarcasm about statecraft. Even the holy war as practiced in the Old Testament is not statecraft as usual. It had no standing army, no generals, no war colleges, and no horses or chariots. Holy war was a miracle when it happened. It could truly be said that God gave the victory to his people. After the kingship experiment runs its course, Isaiah and Jeremiah finally say, "Told you so. That model was never what God really wanted, so we are going to do it the other way again. We are going to do it Abraham's way. We are going to live by faith and let God be our only king."

So when Jesus creates an alternative community, he is not doing something new. He simply updates and reaffirms what had been going on since Abraham. It is no surprise that we are told three different times in the New Testament that to be a child of Abraham is to believe in Jesus. We find it in the Baptist's preaching (Matthew 3:9), John's gospel (John 8:31-47), and Paul's letters (Galatians 3:7). Jesus is doing Abraham's thing again. He reconstitutes God's people around God's alternative vision. We do not have to be our own lords because God is our king.

Jesus did not address individuals with the message that if you get your head and heart right you will function better in society as an individual, as a citizen, and as a professional in your field. Nor did Jesus bring a vision of a new society that could be imposed from the top down. He did not bring a new constitution, a new set of laws, or new way to regulate global economic and social structures. What Jesus brought was a new way of being a distinctive and set-apart people.

Discerning our place in world history

To appreciate the new way of being God's people that Jesus brought, we can make a typology of the social options available to God's people during his time and consider how they relate to the options before us now. Four people groups in his society represent four logical ways to go about setting things right. All of these groups cared deeply about God's people and none of them was irresponsible.

One group of people in Jesus' world was the Sadducees. Sometimes we find them linked with the Herodians. They tried to make the best of a bad situation. They knew that the Romans were there for a long time and that they could not be gotten rid of by fighting back. We tend to look at these people negatively, but they were not scoundrels or collaborators. They were responsible community leaders doing the best they could to preserve Jewish identity under Roman occupation, and they did so fairly well. They got the Romans to promise not to bring idolatrous banners into Jerusalem. When the Roman army came to Jerusalem, they left their flags behind so as not to offend the anti-idolatry convictions of the Jews. The Sadducees also gained permission to use special coins to pay the temple tax. This spared the temple from being profaned by idolatrous images on coins that bore Caesar's name. By clever political negotiation, they obtained religious freedom for Jews. In the whole Roman Empire, Jews were the only group that did not have to worship Caesar. The Sadducees therefore represent the option of exercising responsibility for society by making the best of a bad deal and working within the establishment. This was an intelligent, honorable strategy during Jesus' time.

On the other end of the spectrum were the Zealots. These were the national liberation front of Jesus' time. They knew that the Romans could not be appealed to by humane calls to decency. They would only understand violence, so the Zealots responded to them on their own terms. This meant attempting to drive them out with righteous violence. It has been said that every year somebody was put to death in Galilee for trying this from before Jesus' time until AD 135. There were several revolutions and they were always eventually suppressed by the Romans. Nonetheless, the Zealots insisted that with God's power and perhaps the help of angels, they could do again what the Maccabees had once done—set up a righteous kingdom, drive out the pagans, and purify the temple. This, too, was a responsible option in Jesus' day, albeit a very different strategy.

There were others who did not approve of the Sadducees or Zealots because of their impure tactics. The Essenes believed that only God would save Israel and only after they were ready for salvation. How did they get ready? They had to repent, discipline themselves, and form faithful communities outside Jerusalem. They went to the desert—not because they were indifferent about Jerusalem, but because they cared enormously about Jerusalem and its pollution by pagans. Only God could help, and when God acted they would be ready to take over the temple. In the meantime, they petitioned God to act by praying regularly, remaining faithful, studying Scripture, and waiting for divine intervention.

The fourth group is the Pharisees, which means "separatists." They did not migrate physically but culturally. They kept working, making money, gathering crops, and doing business in society. But they had very clear lines about involving themselves with the Romans. For example, they could not touch a royal coin or handle polluted objects. The Pharisees developed their lifestyle around discipline and purity in order to maintain faithfulness to God in the midst of a broader social and economic life.

You can try these four options in any culture. You can disavow a culture and withdraw until it collapses. You can strive to destroy the present order with righteous revolution. You can shrewdly work against the system from within it. Or you can draw certain lines to remain clean in a world you cannot change. These are the four things you can do when you are in an unacceptable situation, but Jesus did not do any of them. It matters, though, that they did not all have equal weight for him. He did not simply dump them all. We have no indication that he was ever tempted to be a Sadducee, as most of us are. We do not know of his being tempted to stay in the desert, although his relationship to John the Baptist and the wilderness setting of the temptation narratives might indicate that he had some awareness of those who do. But he did not retreat; he set his face toward Jerusalem and consciously went to where the power and the problems were.

Jesus talked more with the Pharisees than with anybody else, according to the Gospels. That fact makes us think they were the bad guys, but that would be a misreading of the text and even more so of the wider social context. The Pharisees were closer to Jesus than the previous two groups. That is why they could argue so much with each other. They lived in the same universe of discourse, had the same concerns, and stood against many of the same things. Jesus was part of the Pharisaic movement in his concern for the law of God, righteousness, and obedience. He even recommends doing what the Pharisees say, just not what they do—or at least not the way they were doing it (Matthew 23:3). He was part of their movement in terms of teaching. But his way of calling people to follow him differed from their way of calling people to keep clean. We should note, then, that when the Pharisees work with the Sadducees—their natural enemies—to get rid of Jesus, this is a highly unusual collaboration.

The fourth position, the righteous revolution of the Zealots, is the temptation closest to Jesus. One of his disciples is even named Simon the Zealot. Some scholars have suggested that as many as half of the twelve disciples were of Zealot background. These were the people Jesus attracted. He spoke their language: he talked about total commitment, the wrongness of the present system, and God's intention to make things right. Jesus sounded so much like a Zealot that many of his disciples thought he was one. In the upper room they thought he was going to establish a Zealot kingdom, so they squabbled about who would sit at his right hand. Jesus was so much like a Zealot that he was put to death by the Romans on the grounds that he was king of the Jews. The inscription on a Roman cross states the nature of a criminal's offense, so as to deter all onlookers from repeating it. Jesus' placard read "king of the Jews." Though Pilate knew that was not the whole story, it was still the legal reason for his crucifixion. He was a Zealot, an insurgent, a threat to the throne.

Even though Jesus was not a Zealot, he was willing to be misunderstood as one. He was willing to come so close to that image that he could die because of it. Nevertheless, he was not a Zealot. That option was doomed to defeat (which happened in AD 70 and 130), but that is not why Jesus turned it down. He turned it down because it was not the way of the suffering servant. It was not the way to be God's chosen one in this world.

But if Jesus did not take any of the four ways mentioned above, then what did he do? He planted a people. He started a new human movement that had a different way of dealing with offenders, underdogs, outsiders, money, leadership, and decision making. Even if Jesus' followers were feeble, confused, and scattered, they nonetheless lived out a new social option. In the New Testament vision, that option is what carries the meaning of history. History is not what the globally visible structures of empire are doing. The meaning of history is what God is doing in this new people.

The most dramatic vision of this is in Revelation 4–5. John sees a vision of the heavenly courtroom in which God is enthroned with a sealed scroll in hand. This scroll is the key to things. It contains the plan, the divine mystery, the secret of history, but no one can open it. No one has the power and moral authority to open the scroll and grasp what destiny is all about. John weeps until he is informed of one who is worthy to open the scroll. He then sees the slain Lamb, and the heavenly hosts sing a new song—a song about the meaning of history, about the answers to John's questions as he sits on a desert island wondering where God's victory is. That meaning is then revealed. It is the work of the Lamb to gather a new people: "You are worthy to take the scroll and to open its seals, for you were slaughtered and by your blood you ransomed for God saints from every tribe and language and people and nation; you have made them to be a kingdom and priests serving our God, and they will reign on earth" (Revelation 5:9-10). There is our phrase again. What God is doing in history is gathering a new people from around the land. That is the meaning of world history.

Caesar thought that what he was doing was the meaning of world history. John knew that what the *church* was doing was the meaning of world history. The early church used theological language to express this: Jesus Christ is Lord. We tend to pietize and spiritualize the word *Lord*. In our usage, whether Christ is Lord has come to mean whether I make him my Lord. Yet the lordship of Christ is his relationship to the universe, not just to us. It is his relationship to the principalities and powers, to the meaning of all history. That is what the New Testament means when it says Christ is Lord.

The early Christians did not care about individual salvation as much as we do, but they did care about where God is taking the world. They said two things about world history. They said that the real meaning of history is the gathering of this new people of every tribe and tongue and nation. They also said that the risen Lord sits at the right hand of the Father, far above the rest of the world—including Caesar, the Persians, the principalities and powers, and the angelic world. He is above them all even if we cannot see how. There is the visible community gathered around the Lamb, and there is the invisible sovereignty of God with Christ seated at the right hand. This distinction between the visible and invisible is crucial because it does not take long before God's people begin to lose it.

Losing our place in world history

A fundamental shift in history between Scripture and our time is represented by the fourth-century emperor Constantine, who converted to Christianity and took the Roman Empire along with him. Constantine is a symbol. There are biographical discussions about how sincere he was, whether he was really converted, and why he did not accept baptism until shortly before dying. But the shift symbolized by Constantine did not simply take place with the man Constantine and his edict of toleration. It took at least a century of change and compromise before theology could support the Constantinian settlement. Long before Constantine, Christians had become pro-empire and anti-Jewish. It did not all just flip in the year 311 or 320; there was already evolution in this direction.

Nevertheless, several shifts eventually take place. To begin with, there is a shift in ethics. If Constantine is the chief member of the church, then we are going to have to be in favor of war instead of against it. That shift happened, and it is well documented in the histories of Christian ethics. There will also have to be a shift in the meaning of the church. If the whole culture is now Christian by virtue of the fact that the emperor is a Christian, then everyone is Christian by default. Baptizing babies born into the empire, and thus into Christianity, begins to make sense. When this became the norm, everyone was automatically considered a Christian as opposed to adults making a decision based on hearing a message.

Beneath the shift in the nature of the church and the nature of Christian ethics is a shift in salvation history. In other words, there is a difference in what God is doing in the world. Before Constantine, you knew there existed a church, a people of God, and you took it on faith that God ruled the universe. After Constantine, you knew for sure that God was ruling the universe—just look at Constantine—but you had to take it on faith that there was a church.

At this point, Augustine develops the doctrine of the invisibility of the church. You do not really know who is a believer, but we baptize everybody. Baptism no longer correlates with faith. Some people behave and some do not. Pagans can behave well and believers can behave badly, so there is really no way to know what the true church is. Since the true church is invisible, we will have to make do with the visible church, which is not the true church. There is also a fundamental shift in where God is working to save the world. Before Constantine, there is a visible people of God and an invisible providence. After Constantine, there is a visible providence and an invisible people of God. That is a fundamental structural shift in how to see history and reality.

The Reformation and elements of modernity have tried to correct this. Reformers like Luther and Calvin criticized the Roman Catholic Church's view of justification, sacraments, and church organization. Those criticisms are correct, but few people challenged the deeper issue of the Constantinian arrangement itself. The meaning of membership in the Christian community, the linkage of church and state as institutions, the place for violence in defense of the Christian culture—these are things that only a few radical reformers would question.

Anglo-Saxon democracy, for its part, has changed the meaning of "establishment." Even though there is no official establishment of religion in modern democracies, the notion of establishment is still very much our mood. You can separate the church as institution from the state as institution and yet the church can still serve as chaplain to the establishment. So it remains common in our time for people to think and live more from the heritage of Constantine than not.

Twenty years ago, John Smylie wrote a brief but significant article: "The Christian Church and the National Ethos." Smylie argued that the nation is, for many of us, more the "chosen people" than the church. Or to say it the other way, the nation is the believing community for many of us. This has happened in three ways.

First, the nation became the primary agent of God's meaningful activity in history. The Americanization of the whole world became the obvious goal of history. The nation became the chosen people of God and replaced the community of the redeemed as the new Israel. Historically, we got this from two sources: from the Old Testament patterns brought into New England and from romantic views of history that made nations the significant units of history.

Second, the nation replaces the church by becoming the primary society in which individuals find personal identity. The nation is the new unity that absorbs all pluralities and enables realization of one's personal life. The individualism and pluralism of North America sometimes blind us to the overriding unity and homogeneity that makes everything the same here. I get who I am from the nation, not from the people with whom I am a disciple.

Third, the nation became the primary community that defines historic purpose and identity. It took over the church's function as the community of righteousness. In other words, the nation can police our morality and the church cannot anymore. For instance, most Christians today would not want the church to know how much money they make, but they would say that the government has a right to know. They would not want their church to ask neighbors about their personal lives, but the FBI can. It is widely recognized now that we live in an age when people assume that the nation is the bearer of the meaningful work of God in history.

Recovering our place in world history

This stands in stark contrast with the gospel. The ethics of Jesus both enables and presumes a different community as the bearer of God's work in history. This community is fundamentally different in its perception of and commitment to what God wants to do in the world. This is not just an alternative that arises out of contemporary experience. For some people, moral insight must be new, and new is usually better. They like the notion of a counter cultural community because it happens to be the newest thing.

For others, moral insight stems from historical lessons that have to be proven in and through history. If the Constantinian settlement collapses under its own weight, then we should ask whether it was overcentralized or out of balance. If our gas-guzzling culture turns out to be unsustainable in the long run, then we should question the assumption that all the world's resources are ours to spend. We learn these things only after that fact. If Richard Nixon cheats, then we will become a little more skeptical about the virtues of people in high places. If the most powerful military in the world cannot beat back guerillas in Vietnam, we will raise doubts about how much of our culture the Pentagon should run. These experiences teach us that our assumptions are often wrong. And it is good to learn about wrong assumptions from bad experiences.

But if theology matters, gospel is good news, and revelation is real, then we have to come to grips with the fact that we always knew these things. Worldly power was never usable for reconciliation even when some people thought it was. The resources of the world were never ours to waste, even when they seemed limitless to us. The Constantinian approach to running the world was never what Jesus wanted his followers to do. What God wants goes all the way back to Abraham and was renewed in Jesus and the people of Pentecost. The thing that matters most to the God of all creation is to send a special people into the world whose identity and dignity is precisely their differentness, their otherness. They are not to be different simply for the sake of difference, but because they desire to be God's instrument and to be like God's Son in a world that even God is too nonviolent to control except by suffering at its hands.

7

God's People and the State[1]

The purpose of this essay is to understand why it is proper for Christians to witness to the state about how the state should fulfill its function as a state. But before we enter this discussion, let us note that there are only a few Christians for whom it needs to be discussed. Most Christians and non-Christians alike have no reservations about serving the state, administering it, and seeking power within it. For them, speaking to the state raises no ethical questions. There is nothing wrong with discussing problems that one is willing to participate in fixing. The question of speaking to the state becomes especially important when faced by persons who, for reasons of conviction, do not participate in executing the decisions they discuss. If one had an all-volunteer army, for example, we might ask whether conscientious objectors should speak to an issue in which they were not directly involved. Is this logical and proper?

---

1. This chapter was originally published as "Things That Are Caesar's, Part 1," *Christian Living* (July 1960): 4–5, 34; "Things That Are Caesar's, Part 2," *Christian Living* (August 1960): 14–17, 39; "Things That Are Caesar's, Part 3," *Christian Living* (September 1960): 16–18. For those interested in further reading on the topics addressed in this chapter, see John Howard Yoder, *The Christian Witness to the State* (Scottdale, PA: Herald Press, 2002).

Christ is Lord

The fundamental confession of faith of the early church is summed up in three words: "Christ is Lord." We use this phrase so much in our religious vocabulary that we can repeat it without knowing what we say. The apostles believed in the divine sonship of Christ, but first and foremost they proclaimed his lordship. They believed in his miraculous birth, his teachings, and his expected return, but they preached "our Lord reigns!" At Pentecost, Peter proclaimed, "God has made him both Lord and Messiah!" (Acts 2:36). In Philippians 2:11, Paul says, "Every tongue should confess that Jesus Christ *is* Lord!"

"Let us crown him Lord of all!" is the refrain of a well-loved hymn. The sentiment is fine, but the doctrine is not quite complete. Christ is Lord. It is not up to us to crown him, but only to acknowledge his sovereignty. If we do not acknowledge this—if we keep on being our own masters, whether as individuals, social groups, or nations—that changes nothing of the reality or the permanence of his lordship. It simply means that we shall one day break ourselves on the rock on which we have refused to build. Christ is King, and his dominion is eternal. Since his resurrection and exaltation to the right hand of God, he is reigning, even though death and his other enemies have not yet been fully brought into subjection. "For he must reign until he has put all his enemies under his feet" (1 Corinthians 15:25).

Is this the poetic language of pious enthusiasm, or does it have something to do with the state and with specific problems of political ethics? The first Christians were convinced that among the "thrones, dominions, principalities, and powers" against whom they waged spiritual warfare were the heads and the agents of civil government. They believed that by virtue of his lordship God was using these "powers" to achieve certain of his purposes. Fallen powers could be God's servants for our good (Romans 13:4). By maintaining the peace they facilitate humanity's coming to the knowledge of the truth (1 Timothy 2:2-4).

Even though the powers that are at work in the world, including the state, may not serve Christ on the level of deliberate voluntary discipleship, they can still be used in his service and for his glory. This has traditionally been spoken of as providence. By referring to it instead as Christ's lordship or kingship, the New Testament relates it more clearly to Christ's ministry and triumph of the passion and resurrection. This also makes clear that we are called to participate in willing fellowship with Christ and obedience to Christ.

Making his lordship known

This does not yet answer the question we have been asking. Christ rules over the nations without their necessarily knowing it, and his doing so is not dependent on our assistance. Why then should we speak to the state? Should state and church each let the other go its own way?

We are told in Ephesians 3:10 that the church should proclaim God's plan to the powers. The faithful church should always be doing this. For example, when the apostle Paul appeared before the authorities, he called upon them to respect his legal privileges as a citizen. Christian faithfulness involves having only one primary loyalty. When the empire or nation asks to be put first, Christians must give an account and explain why they cannot fully conform. In this testimony there is always an implied criticism of the state's practice. By refusing to perform military service they testify against all war, even though they do not expect that the state will disarm. Christians who refuse to participate in idolatry speak at first glance only for themselves. In reality they challenge the state's right to force its subjects to religious conformity. When Christians throughout history have argued for religious liberty and against persecution, they were being consistent with this line of the original witness.

Christian witness usually asks whether the demands the state is making lie within its authority. We are not called to submit to every demand of every state. When Paul instructs the Roman Christians to give "taxes to whom taxes are due, revenue to whom revenue is due, respect to whom respect is due, honor to whom honor is due" (Romans 13:7), this is the opposite of saying that tax, revenue, respect, and honor are due the state. He is saying, as the similarities to Matthew 22:21 and 1 Peter 2:17 confirm, that we are to make a distinction and give to each only what they are due. We must never give to Caesar what belongs to God.

Our brother's keeper

It is possible to see, from another direction, why Christians should testify to governments and social leaders. Christ has not commanded us to love our neighbors simply for the sake of obedience to God or helpfulness to others. Christ has told us that in serving the neighbor we serve him. A loving deed toward other people is the only way we can in fact serve him. "No one has ever seen God" except in his brother or sister (1 John 4:12).

If we are concerned for the welfare of others, we will speak whenever injustice threatens them, legal or otherwise. If society prevents others from being housed, clothed, or fed decently, we owe it to them to name and denounce that evil and to help them recover from any ill treatment. When Nazism was persecuting the Jews, it was not enough to provide hospitality for refugees. The evil itself had to be denounced as a sin against God and humanity. The same is the case for war, racial discrimination, exploitation of the poor, and a host of other offenses against the dignity of humans whom God loves.

Yet to denounce evil always implies that those who do evil could have done good, or at least better. Witnessing against evil involves some notion of the preferable alternatives. To condemn partiality means that we are calling for honesty and justice according to certain standards. To condemn the bombing of Coventry by the Germans or Hiroshima by the Americans raises the question of what governments should have done.

The witness already being given

Even if it could not be proven with complete certainty that it is the Christian's duty to "speak truth to power," we shall keep on speaking. Even our silence communicates. Whether we vote or refuse to vote, we are saying something. Our participation in the economy, in the school system, in the market for newspapers and magazines, already speaks volumes. The difference between a witness to government that is explicit and one that we give in spite of ourselves by our silence is not a difference between being involved in politics and not being involved. It is a matter of whether we are aware and careful about what we say.

Society's conscience

"You are the salt of the earth. . . . You are the light of the world. A city built on a hill cannot be hid" (Matthew 5:13-14). In the images that Jesus uses, a small part affects the whole. A lamp shares its light with the whole room, even though only a small amount of oil is caught up in the flame. The city on a hill provides orientation and perspective to people who never actually make a pilgrimage up that hill. The salt flavors and preserves without transforming the whole dish into salt. In the same way, as a by-product to her central task, the Christian church will radiate a moral influence on the world around it, including the state.

But knowing that we have good reason to speak to the state is only part of the problem. Knowing what we should say is still more difficult. Because they are afraid of saying the wrong thing, many Christians who are deeply concerned about suffering and injustice have remained silent.

When Christians speak against the draft and thereby indirectly in favor of a professional army and greater reliance on new weapons, how can we be sure this is the advice the government needs? Many Christians voted for the prohibition of alcohol and called for governmental suppression of obscene literature through the postal service. Can we be sure that forcing the vices of alcoholism and pornography to "go underground" did not in fact make them more harmful and harder to control? These examples illustrate the fear of saying the wrong thing, even when the Christian position seems quite clear.

Our basic message is the call to repentance and faith. Christ judges us, calls us to turn, and gives us the power of the Spirit to walk in newness of life. This message is so clear that even those who reject the message he brought generally agree about what it meant. But what we need to tell the state cannot be this clear. For the state, insofar as it bears the sword, exists only "outside the perfection of Christ."[2] The state exists because of sin and its agents are people who have decided, at least for the present, not to act in the non-resistant, self-giving way we call discipleship. If all we say to agents of the state is that they should follow Christ, they may well understand the evangelistic appeal, but they will not see how this applies to their work. If they understand anything, it will be that their office as agent of the state should no longer exist, which is not, on the basis of the Bible, exactly what we want to say.

It is therefore quite understandable that many Christians have seen this as one place where a double standard must be used. This position has taken many different forms in traditional Catholicism, Lutheranism, Calvinism, and various forms of fundamentalism. It is understood that God has two distinct wills—one for the Christian in the church and another for the unbeliever in society at large, especially in the state. God actively and effectively desires that the state should use violence and that the Christian should not. God's will here is not only permissive, as is the case for the fall of humanity into sin. God so desires that the state should bear the sword that Christians who suggest that it might do so a little less destructively are believed to be working against God's will. God so desires the death of a murderer, according to this view, that for a governor to pardon someone or for Christians to ask the governor to do so means that the state is being unfaithful to its divine mandate.

This "double standard" position has had many advocates throughout church history and is advocated today by Christians whose testimony deserves a wide hearing. This chapter attempts to explain a position that is more consistent with the New Testament. It is intended to open discussion, not close it down.

To you for good

One of the generally accepted ideas of modern religious liberalism has been its high respect for human personality.

---

2. Yoder is here citing a phrase from the Schleitheim Confession, a statement that was adopted by Swiss Anabaptists in 1527.

The "dignity of humanity" has been made the basic religious value, and on this foundation it has been possible to argue in favor of democracy, the Bill of Rights, trial by jury, and social welfare measures. This assumption that humanity is basically good is a theological error if nothing is said of the effects of the fall on human nature and human status before God. Yet for Christians there is a sense in which it is true that human dignity is a basic moral value. All humans, even the morally unworthy ones, have a real value before God. They possess this value not by their own merits but by virtue of Christ. Jesus was not carelessly exaggerating when he said, "inasmuch as you did *it* to one of the least of these My brethren, you did it to Me" (Matthew 25:40 NKJV). Because of Christ, my neighbor's welfare is my concern.

One way to express this concern is to remind the agents of the state that they are obliged to act "for good" (Romans 13:4). They must act within the limits of respect for human welfare and personal dignity, even of the unworthy. Police should be reminded that even a criminal must be treated decently and humanely. Prison authorities and government officials responsible for prison facilities need to be reminded that their prisoners are human beings. Facilities that do not separate hardened criminals from first-time juvenile delinquents are an offense against human dignity that Christians should not want to see in their country.

This concern for human welfare may express itself in numerous ways, including what we say about the economic order, social welfare agencies, schools, taxes, overseas aid, and connections between the police and the underworld. Yet one of the clearest and most direct points at which it arises is the state's assumption that it has the right, or even the duty, to kill certain social offenders. Capital punishment is increasingly seen as not only unchristian but socially unjustified.[3] It is useless to repress crime and it serves as a source of inequality and wasted effort in the courts. Christians should not leave all initiative in this area to pragmatic criminologists and humanistic religious leaders. Christians should bear witness to executioners and judges that the lives they take are not really theirs to take.

---

3. This is not as true in the United States today as it was when Yoder wrote this.

The Old Testament authorized the death penalty, though less broadly than the pagan moral codes of Moses' time. The Old Testament also authorized divorce, polygamy, genocide, and the stoning of rebellious children. Since Christ died the death which all people earned by their sin, the sacrifice for the sin of murder (Genesis 9:6) has been fulfilled "once for all" just like all the other dimensions of sacrificial system (Hebrews 7:27; 9:28; 10:10). The prophetic message that God does not desire the death of the sinner (Ezekiel 18:23; 33:11) is not only "spiritual" in its meaning.[4]

If a state government ceases to put criminals to death, this does not mean that the world will be basically changed or that all problems regarding the treatment of criminals will be solved. To testify against one evil or in favor of one humane act of the state need not involve utopian illusions about the world's betterment. Our motivation is not that we expect to save society, but that the person whose welfare is at stake is one of "the least of these" (Matthew 25:40).

Every knee shall bow

Going beyond this general concern for human welfare, we may look at several other principles to govern our testimony to the state. One of these grows out of understanding sin most basically as pride. The state not only protects society against some of the effects of sin, it is also one of the most obvious ways that human pride expresses itself. This may be expressed in the desire of one person to dominate others, which is one of the traits of all human government (Matthew 20:25). It may even go so far as open idolatry when a state or individual ruler actually claims absolute religious significance (Revelation 13). In these extreme situations, the Christian path is called "the endurance and faith of the saints" (Revelation 13:10), that is, the witness of non-resistant suffering, even to the point of death.

---

4. For a collection of Yoder's writings on capital punishment, see *The End of Sacrifice: The Capital Punishment Writings of John Howard Yoder*, edited by John C. Nugent (Harrisonburg, VA: Herald Press, 2011).

There is no reason to assume that the Christian testimony against a state which deifies itself should be limited to these extreme situations. A government that does not persecute Christians and does not ask to be openly worshiped in some ritualistic way is subject to the temptation of pride in other forms. This pride should be denounced as part of the total Christian witness to Christ's lordship.

The Christian witness should then call for limitations upon the exercise of state power within the legal order. The most extreme case is that of persecution. Christians throughout the ages have proclaimed that persecution itself is not the proper function of the state. Yet once again this should not be limited to the extreme case. The democratic institutions of trial by jury, habeas corpus, the checks and balances system, and the respect for a constitution that limits state authority are all indirect expressions of the impact that the Christian witness has had on the life of the state for nearly two thousand years. Such institutions did not arise in parts of the world where the Christian witness was not represented. The very idea of a constitution serving as a control upon the authority of those in high places has not been produced by Islam, Confucianism, Hinduism, or any other religious tradition.

This means that in our own time one of the subjects concerning which the Christian witness to the state must always be vigilant is the responsibility of those in power to respect the limitations of their office and everything involved in the due process of law. The self-restraint that such considerations impose upon those in government does not make them Christians, but it makes them better state authorities, which is preferable for the church and the world.

Christian internationalism

When the New Testament speaks of "Caesar" this is not to be understood as a direct equivalent of the modern nation-state. As far as many of the subjects of the Roman Empire were concerned, Caesar represented the government of the whole world. This was, of course, not literally true. But the conditions of communication being what they were, there were real grounds for equating the Roman Empire with "all the world" as the New Testament does in Luke 2:1. Thus when the Bible speaks of the legitimacy of government and names "Caesar" as representative of that concept, it is not speaking of local governments that are limited to one province or nation and set up in opposition to other local or national governments. Rather it is speaking of the principle of government as it is exercised over the "whole world" by Rome.

This means that there is one aspect of the modern state for which there is no warrant in the Bible: the selfish local interest that a nation is dedicated to preserving. In our age it is almost assumed that the purpose of government includes protecting the selfish interests of its population and rulers against those of other nations. This is not "Caesar's" assignment in Scripture.

Thus Christians have a responsibility to challenge nationalism wherever it becomes clear that a nation-state is defending not simply law and order but the selfish interests of its inhabitants over against those of other nations. That such national selfishness should be condemned does not mean that Christians will always have an easy answer to the question of what the authorities should do differently. Nevertheless, the denunciation of national selfishness is part of the Christian testimony to the state as it is, in favor of the state as it should be. When we challenge national selfishness, we are not challenging the state—we are calling the local state to be what the state should be in principle. It should be an organ of justice and equality rather than selfishness.

One of the most obvious expressions of national selfishness is war. There may have been times when one could argue that wars were actually for the sake of preserving the state itself, and thereby legitimate. This is not the place to debate that issue. It is quite clear, however, that in modern warfare the state or states that prepare for and carry on military hostilities are drawn away from their God-ordained function of maintaining internal order.

The nation that prepares and wages war weakens its economy, diverts qualified persons from positions of social leadership, and runs the risk of actually being destroyed. Instead of protecting the innocent from the wicked, it causes the innocent to suffer and encourages the violent. So when we testify to the state that modern warfare is wrong, we are not speaking only of the fact that Christians should not bear arms. We are saying that warfare is not the task of the state as defined by the New Testament (see Romans 13:1-7; 1 Peter 2:13-17; 1 Timothy 2:2). When we testify against national selfishness, nuclear testing, and biological and chemical weapons, we are speaking not against but for the state which God has ordained.[5]

I do not present the above issues with the notion that they are all desirable or that they have been spelled out with sufficient clarity so that Christians should immediately act without further study. They are, however, valid as examples of the kind of thing which Christians may be called to do if they take seriously the testimony of Scripture that Christ is Lord over worldly authorities, which he uses in spite of their rebellion to accomplish his ends. If the people whom government either threatens or protects are my brothers and sisters, if "righteousness exalts a nation" (Proverbs 14:34), and if Christ truly sits at the right hand of God, having drawn into his triumphal procession the principalities and powers through the victory of the cross (Colossians 1:15), then the church and the world are on different levels—not in separate compartments.

Our proclamation of the righteousness of God includes both telling people how to be saved and telling the authorities how to be just. We would be unfaithful if we were to place the second of these before the first, but the fact that it is secondary does not make it undesirable. When concern for the mistreatment of the working classes is left to the Marxists, when the denunciation of imperialism is left to Gandhian Hindus, when the struggle against racial segregation in the United States is left largely to humanistic groups, when moral initiative is taken up by non-Christian groups, this is a sign of the church's infidelity and a judgment on her silence. Christians have also been unfaithful to their Lord by leaving secondary things undone.

---

5. At this point in the original manuscript, Yoder devotes several paragraphs to the topic of economic selfishness in the form of protective tariffs. His ultimate point is that Christians need to work against selfishness not only in issues of war but in economics as well. We have cut it in keeping with the aims of this volume and refer those who are interested in what Yoder says here to "Things That Are Caesar's, Part 2," *Christian Living* (August 1960), 17, 39.

The other side

Another way that Christians need to be faithful is through listening carefully to the other side. In this divided world the cause of the "other side" seldom gets a fair hearing. Castro and Khrushchev, powerful as they are within their own realms, are open to attacks, distorted reporting, and defamation within the United States with no one to check the extent of the abuse.

Without approving of Khrushchev's or Castro's methods, Christians can at least remind their critics to compare their regimes with their predecessors rather than with Anglo-Saxon traditions of democracy. We can ask whether the pressure tactics of North American diplomacy did not contribute to what authoritarian rulers can get away with. This reminder is especially clear when "our side" has contributed to the escalation of tensions and refuses to accept the blame for doing so.

In a sense, Christians should always be "on the other side," ambassadors for the absent. This does not mean that the other side is blameless or less blameworthy than "our side." It is simply a corrective in view of our side's tendency to selfish unfairness. Each nation assumes the validity of a double standard in its own favor. When American planes fly over Russia, this is explained as the Russians' fault for not permitting free movement of investigators. Yet America proclaims to the world that the first Russian plane over North America will set off retaliatory missiles against Moscow. We build and arm air bases in Turkey and Pakistan, yet if the Russians send so much as a trade mission to Cuba, it is denounced as a threat to the peace of the whole Western Hemisphere.

In reality, the double standard should apply in the other way. If the West claims any allegiance to higher standards of morality, respect for law, and truthfulness, then the sincerity of this claim will be tested by whether these standards are applied more critically and lived up to more fully on our side. The French expression *noblesse oblige* (nobility obliges) conveys the idea that those who claim greater moral worth thereby lay on themselves greater obligations. This is a general principle of moral insight that Christians should apply.

The state in modern times

One major difficulty in applying Christian witness to the state today is the broad scope of what the modern state actually does. Caesar was practically a dictator. Today people govern themselves through constitutional and democratic means. Caesar's primary function, apart from keeping himself in power, was maintaining social order. The state in our day teaches children, supports the poor, provides for the aged, prepares for the destruction of the race with nuclear and bacterial weapons, carries the mail, builds dams, and sells electricity. In many parts of the world it builds the factories and markets the crops.

Caesar governed the known world. Today the world is divided into a hundred sovereign nations, some bound together in commonwealths, some subdivided into relatively independent states, some just coming into being, and others centuries old. You could always tell who Caesar was and who his representatives were. Today there may be two states claiming to govern the same population. Examples include the puppet governments in Europe during the Cold War, the "governments in exile" during Hitler's time, the conflicting powers in a civil war, the conflict between state and federal demands in the integration issue, or the conflict between the UN and some of its member nations on human rights. Caesar persecuted the Christians and sometimes asked to be honored as a God. Governments today may call themselves Christian or, if officially neutral, at least respect the churches and even subsidize them. They even count Christians among their highest officials.

It is naive to argue that these great changes make no difference in the spiritual significance of the state. Is teaching in a university or serving as a social worker today the same as fighting in the Roman army in Jesus' time since both are dependent on the state? Yet if the changes are so sweeping, is there nothing left to guide us but a few vague generalities or the arbitrary whims of "conscience" or "common sense"?

Christians always seem to choose one of these extremes. Some have been so struck by the changes, especially the coming of democracy and favoring of Christianity as a religion, that they see the life of the New Testament church as of no help in our day. They think we should be guided by secular views of "peace" and "justice" and keep our religion inside the individual. Others, with a strong confidence in the clarity and solidity of words, would be so sure that the "state" is always the "state" that they will speak in one breath of the United States president and the "avenger of blood" in the Old Testament laws (Numbers 35:19). For them the rightness of modern state warfare is part of Caesar's "not bearing the sword in vain" (Romans 13:4).

Both of these extremes result from the failure to be critical about the meaning of the word "state"—a word that the Bible does not use. The Bible speaks of "the authorities" or of "the sword." These terms point not to an organization with multiple functions, but to one particular function: the wielding of coercive power in the interest of order. If this is what we mean by "state" and we watch our words carefully then it is clear that there will always be a state and that its function is not one to which the Christian disciple is called. Yet let us not be hasty in concluding which other services and activities in the modern "state" are also excluded.

Responsibility within government

This warning against hasty confusion of separate realities is especially needed when we approach the possibility of the Christian's involvement in social organization. Are Christians doing their duty or shirking it when they fail to vote? This is an opportunity today's "Caesar" offers to influence the choice of political leaders, but the one in Rome did not. Some argue that voting is part and parcel of the state system, so that the voter is morally involved in all that the state does, including bearing the sword. Others argue that the vote is a product of the Christian influence on society over the years and that to fail to assist in the choice of the most qualified and honest leaders is to cast a passive vote for corruption.

Both of these views are confusing because they oversimplify. On the one hand, the "whole system" argument—whereby the soldier, executive, legislator, office worker, and voting citizen are all morally on the same level—is unreasonable. The noncombatant soldier is not the same as the combatant soldier. If the Christian conscientious objector refuses both kinds of military service, it is because both are objectionable, not because one is polluted by the other. If being "part of the system" means the same degree of moral blame, then in modern total warfare the taxpayer, farmer, schoolteacher, and transportation worker are no less involved. To follow this view consistently would make Jesus himself a sinner, for he too was involved in sinful society, its economy, its division of labor, and its politics.

It is true that the state is a cohesive system, just as the fallen world is a cohesive realm of the "prince of the power of the air" (Ephesians 2:2 KJV). Yet Christ's victory enables us to victoriously inhabit the world without being of the world. The systems and structures of the world (modern terms for what the Bible calls "principalities and powers") have been disarmed by the cross and deprived of their capacity to dominate. There is room for freedom in their midst— freedom to do and say the right thing here and now without fearing "guilt by involvement."

Those who feel that the coming of democratic theories of government has changed the whole nature of the state over-simplify matters just as seriously. Theories may have changed, but the fact that the many are governed by the few is the same. The vote may be a more direct way for the governed to express their preferences to the rulers, but every government, even a dictatorship, has ways of feeling and respecting the opinion of the people. Moreover, any government, even the most democratic, has ways of ignoring the people's desires. The fact of voting does not necessarily mean that the voter is morally more responsible for the action of the government. In some countries voting is viewed as a citizen's duty and in some cases is compulsory. In other nations it is viewed as a privilege that is limited to people who earn it by their patriotic service or class status. Certainly the vote does not always have the same moral meaning. In many elections no real issue is at stake and most significant government decisions are never brought to a vote.

These observations should free us from a sense of obligation to find blanket answers that call for either uncritical involvement or total withdrawal from social leadership. We participate in government one way or another, whether as voters or nonvoters, candidates for office or passive bystanders whose inactivity is used by someone. This cannot be changed. What can be changed is our awareness of what we are doing so that our actions and abstentions are intelligently guided. Realistically, we shall note that the vote often makes little difference and that the difference between democracies and other forms of government is far less than we are often led to think.

Yet systematic abstention from voting, holding office, or contributing to public opinion and decision making is neither desirable nor possible. We will avoid certain kinds of involvement because our contribution would make little difference and we have more important occupations. Sometimes we avoid involvement because the action called for would be harmful.

We should be aware that there are other means that contribute more to public life than voting does. Consider, for example, the moral education of children, the power of example, and the costly testimony of a minority willing to suffer for its beliefs. But if and when we may be useful, we should help. If society needs and wants moral leadership, social services, or cultural creativity that Christians can provide through the mechanism of what is currently called the state, then we should help, even if we do not bear the sword.

An awareness of the meaning of Christ's lordship on one hand and of the complexity of the realm of Caesar on the other hand can free us for greater faithfulness. Freed from fear of "involvement," we may let ourselves be constrained by love. Freed from dogmas of "responsibility," we may be recommitted to real nonconformity to this world and to a witness in word and work that our Lord reigns.

8

God's People and War[1]

Can there be a just war? To answer that question, we have to look at a broad range of issues. We cannot just give a simplistic answer, such as *yes, no, maybe, or none of the above.* We also have to define what it is we are talking about. If you want to know whether there can be a unicorn, you first have to define it and distinguish it from a rhinoceros or aardvark. You also have to know where you would expect to find one, whether in a park, a medieval tapestry, a poem, or in the mind of God. So first we have to begin with the definitional, historical reporting.

The term *just war* is an ancient one, so we will have to read some history. It is complex in the way it is defined, so we will have to itemize its numerous elements. It is a term whose meaning has changed over time, so we will have to watch it through history. *Just war* is also a logical term, so we will have to look at some ways of reasoning. I will begin with that.

---

1. This chapter was originally published as "Can There Be a Just War?" *Radix* 13 (Sept–Oct, 1981): 3–9. Reprinted by permission from Radix magazine, www.radixmagazine.com. For those interested in further reading on the topics addressed in this chapter, see John Howard Yoder, *When War is Unjust: Being Honest in Just-War Thinking* (Maryknoll, NY: Orbis, 1996).

There are three ways in which it is simple to resolve the moral problem of war. First, you may simply say it is wrong no matter what. We call that pacifism. Second, you may say that you do whatever your government calls for. The moral question is simple: you let somebody else decide, namely, your government. Sometimes that is called fascism, or Machiavellianism, or realism. Third, you may say, at least with regard to certain wars, that they are holy causes and that God wants them waged that way. The wars of Joshua near the beginning of the Old Testament, the Crusades during the Middle Ages, the Islamic *jihad*, and perhaps some kinds of ideological combat are examples. Such military endeavors are undertaken because they are dictated by some transcendent consideration. In those cases, you do not have to look at individual cases, ask about the rights of the adversaries, or measure the details about how it will go.

Beside those three simple answers, there is one complicated historical answer—that is, sometimes war is right and sometimes it is wrong. It is an evil, but it may be a necessary evil under certain circumstances. Then the circumstances must be defined. You have to ask numerous questions. The relative weight of those questions will itself be part of the question. That is the topic of our focus. It is not my own view, but for the sake of theology and church unity I am invested in the integrity of those who hold it.

The group of people who hold this view includes most Christians. It is the stated view of all the major Christian traditions. If you are a Roman Catholic, it has never been stated for you in a creed, but it is the dominant teaching of the great teachers of the church. If you are Lutheran it is in the Augsburg Confession. If you are Presbyterian or Congregationalist it is in the Westminster Confession. If you are Anglican it is in the Thirty-Nine Articles. If you belong to a church that does not have any confessions, you probably still hold this view because it is the way the Western world has been taught to think.

I have to simplify the description, but I will try to do the job of a fair historian rather than a debater. I will try to do it with objectivity as much as I can, rather than investing my presentation with the passion that the problem of war ought properly to provoke.

The criteria for just war

The just war tradition is a set of criteria. It says that war is usually to be avoided as evil, but that it may be a necessary evil under certain circumstances. To know what those circumstances are you need to have yardsticks, so the tradition consists of a set of criteria.

The intention must be good. Intention may sometimes mean the long-range goal. A war must be undertaken for the peace of the world, and not for some less worthy cause. It may also be more subjective: you should not wage war out of hatred or selfishness.

Only a just authority can wage a just war. A bandit or private citizen cannot wage a just war. Only a legitimate governmental agent can.

The cause must be justified. This could be broken down into many subcases.

The means must be limited. This has to do with *how* you wage a war. The means must be limited by the intrinsic rights of some people not to be harmed. That would include immunity for noncombatants as well as neutral or third parties. The means are also limited by stated rights, such as the modern treaties on the conduct of war that have been signed by all civilized nations. Limits are imposed also by the inner logic of proportionality: the war must not do more harm than good.

The war must be winnable. If there is no reasonable likelihood of winning, then it is wrong to wage a war even for a good cause.

It must be a matter of last resort. If there is any other way to obtain a goal without the use of war, then the war is not justified.

This list of six criteria expands on what existed in the fourth and fifth centuries, when Christian thinkers first began developing just war policy. None of the criteria comes out of the blue, as if some theologian thought it would be a good point to add to the list. All the criteria have an intrinsic logic. The logic is that my neighbors, even my enemies, have a right not to be harmed. If I am going to claim the right to harm them, I ought to meet the logical tests that properly examine that claim. In whose name? For what cause? With what intention? Within what limits?

We have to note that the criteria have changed over the centuries. In thinking about this issue, most of us do not deal with change. We simply say that it is the traditional Christian view, but that is too simple and does not properly attend to the actual history.

How the tradition began

The story begins in the Christian Middle Ages, not in the New Testament. Christians did not hold a just war view until the fourth century. At that point, they adjusted to their new situation of no longer being a persecuted minority. Within their membership, they had Caesar himself and most of his soldiers. They also had the sense that they needed to make a workable ethical system that would permit Caesar and his soldiers to keep on winning their wars. They could not be pacifist anymore, yet they would not be totally unquestioning in their support of Caesar. They needed to develop a system of guidelines.

More than we may realize, the acceptance of war by Christians was an exceptional concession. It was not a duty for everyone in the Middle Ages to fight "just wars." Most people were not supposed to fight. Peasants, clergy, and merchants were exempt from battle. Only the prince and his soldiers (who were relatively few) had the right to shed blood, even in a just war. It was a concession by the Christians, not a duty. It would not have been a mortal sin if they killed under those circumstances, but it was never thought of as a glorious thing. It was an exception relegated only to those few people who bore the authority of the civil government.

More important and more easily forgotten is that the acceptance of just war in the Middle Ages was actually part of a much wider peacemaking concern in the medieval church. Peacemaking claimed more time and energy on the part of bishops and popes than did the actual waging of just wars. There was what they called the *truce of God*—periods of time such as Lent or Sundays, when the bishop would decree that there should be no fighting and those limits would be respected. The *peace of God* was a spatial definition—no fighting on church or monastery land, and no fighting in cemeteries. The bishops frequently intervened to make peace between feuding princes. Those kinds of church practices were respected to some extent. Thus, in the Middle Ages, the just war was only the fringe of a wider concern to have less and less war and to resolve most problems in other ways.

We must also recognize that the just war tradition was not an instrument of decision making prior to waging war. The church did not say, "Before you go to war, think about our checklist of six criteria." That is not the way they did morality in the Middle Ages. The center of morality was the confessional. You committed an act, came to confession, and the priest looked up the seriousness of your act in his book. He then determined how long a time you ought to be kept from participating in the sacraments.

The function of the confessional and canon law created the basis for discussing just war. It was thus in the context of "discipline after the fact" that morality was talked about in the Middle Ages. The just war documents are found in the context of manuals for those who heard confessions and in canon law.

The Protestant Reformation

The next observation, rarely noted, is that the Protestant Reformation made major changes in the meaning of the just war tradition. Specifically, the Reformation decreased its capacity to restrain. The tradition's original intent was to restrain the propensity of princes to wage war by asking questions and condemning certain excesses.

The Reformation decreased the capacity of the just war doctrine to restrain in a number of ways. First, the doctrine was given creedal status, which it never had for Roman Catholics. A Roman Catholic can embrace pacifism, reject the just war theory, and not be a heretic. No council or pope ever put forth just war theory as a necessary doctrine. Catholic pacifists like Dan Berrigan and Dorothy Day are not heretics. They cannot be accused of holding to something that the Catholic Church has formally condemned (even if pacifism is a minority). A Lutheran, Anglican, or Presbyterian can be condemned, however, if they do not hold the just war position. It is in the doctrinal confessions of those communions. As a result, the affirmation that "war may be okay" is given more room in Protestantism than in Catholicism.

The Reformation also eliminated the exceptions in a just

war, especially the clergy and most of the common people. In the Catholic view, the clergy are not supposed to fight. A person who has shed blood, even in a just war, has disqualified himself from being a priest. The Reformation did away with the idea that there are religious people with special ethical obligations and that there ought to be standards that apply to some people and not to others. The Reformation put all the same restrictions (but no additional ones) on the clergy that it put on lay people. Protestants want to do away with the idea that the religious or the clergy are morally special. They likewise wish to do away with the idea that a bishop may declare a certain time or place out of bounds for war. Protestants do not want bishops to get into politics that way.

Social changes also limited bishops' authority. The autonomy of civil rulers was substantially increased by the Protestant Reformation. It was, after all, the rulers who reformed the church. Theologians working for the civil rulers in the Reformation churches were less likely to have moral objectivity or distance in criticizing their kings and princes. That stands in contrast to the Roman Catholic bishops, who had a degree of sociological, economic, and moral independence from their kings. The Reformation freed not only the rulers but also nations from the Catholic vision of the unity of Europe as Christendom. The Protestant Reformation itself was to be a cause of religious wars off and on from the 1530s to 1648. So in addition to the other kinds of interests that drive people to war, people now fought because of the differences between Protestants and Catholics.

In Protestantism, we also find the beginning of a theology of revolution. In addition to saying that an established ruler may fight a just war, Protestantism permitted Christians to revolt against established but unjust regimes. This was especially so if freedom to preach the gospel was not present. Although the Protestant Reformation did not intend to innovate the policies of just war, it effectively and profoundly weakened the original intent of the tradition.

Development of the theory

Another set of historical developments that influenced just war concerns is less open to precise dating. From the late

Middle Ages to the present, a Christian cosmopolitan vision increased the desire of some to restrain war and to use just war vocabulary to do so.

Catholic moralists, especially Francisco de Vitoria in the sixteenth century and Francisco Suarez in the seventeenth, thought theologically and rigorously about the rights of the South American Indians. They wrote the first systematic treatises on just war theory, which previously had only been referenced briefly and unsystematically in moral theology. They wrote with a view toward restraining the excesses of Spanish and Portuguese imperialism. They insisted that indigenous populations had rights that should not be trampled on in the colonial interests of their own nation.

The work of Vitoria and Suarez was important primarily because it made the tradition a coherent theory. It could now be found together in a book with a clear outline. But beyond that, their work distinguished between the ideological cause, such as the Crusaders' claim that God sent them to win a war, and the legal justification that the just war position was really about.

Hugo Grotius also did landmark work on just war theory. Although Dutch, he was a diplomat for various royal houses in Europe. He translated the moral just war statements into legal statements. Grotius moved from asking what would be right and wrong ethically to describing the rights and duties of both governments and combatants. His statements were written in such a way that they could be enforced by the courts, used by ambassadors to negotiate armistice, or applied by diplomats to negotiate behind the scenes. Hugo Grotius is known as the father of international law because of his translations from ethics into law.

The notion of international law is itself a secularization of the just war tradition. Humanistic visions of a parliament of nations became another significant development in just war theory. When it was clear that Europe was breaking into a multitude of small but sovereign peoples, no longer part of an empire or accountable to one another, people with a cosmopolitan spirit saw that this could not be right. There had to be some way, they believed, for peoples to create a society of nations the way individuals create a society of individuals in order to live in a civil manner.

The final type of spokesperson for the just war vision is found in the series of popes who have led the Roman Catholic communion since World War I, beginning with Benedict XV. The popes not only spoke as moral teachers to Catholics but they also pastored the world. They were like the pastor of a village who does not decide who is right or wrong as a judge would, but instead pleads with people to use the instruments they have to keep the peace. Their pleas were based on the vision of a growing amount of work being done by agencies in international conciliation.

War becomes total

I have described a number of developments that emphasize restraint of war. Now I turn toward the other direction. Like the Reformation, modern national structures also decrease the room for restraint in warfare, although for a different set of reasons. The simplest way to explain is to say that war is now total. That means several different things.

First, war is total in the sense of support. Everyone in a nation is part of the war effort because of the unity of a modern economy. That was not the case in the Middle Ages. The ordinary peasant may have had a few more taxes to pay because of a long war, but generally the ability of the nation to win the war was not dependent on everyone doing their part. Nor did people have the sense that it was. Today we consider everyone in the nation, even the opponents of the military policies of the government, as still somehow participating in the military cause. That makes a difference as to whom we consider innocent. It also relates to the just war criteria. It makes a difference in what counts as just authority and whether anybody believes in restraint.

War also became total in its support by the citizenship. Even if the medieval peasants had to pay for the extra cost of a war, they did not think it was their cause. They knew it was the prince's cause. Whether the prince won or lost, the peasant would still be a peasant. Peasants had no ideological stake in most wars.

Today the notion of democracy has made a lot of citizens feel that they are partisans, as if they themselves were the government that is fighting for survival. This heightens the emotional identification of many people with their government and changes the meaning of innocence and noncombatancy. It may open room, in some cases, for those in power to exploit citizen support. One could argue that a wise prince would exercise more restraint in going to war than a nation in which politicians, as part of their electoral campaigns, work people up and get momentum started that they cannot be sure of stopping.

Not only has war become total in the way it is supported economically and ideologically, but the stakes have also become total. New weapons and delivery systems make it possible to destroy everybody on the enemy side. That did not begin with nuclear war, although the nuclear threshold has made it more visible. The possibility of doing more than dealing a decisive blow—that of actually destroying the other nation—goes beyond what the just war tradition used to justify in proportionality and intention.

The stakes are total in still another way. Just as the feeling of the citizen that "our war is my war" has changed since Napoleon, the stakes in the war have changed. Why do we wage wars? Often it is for something like "the very existence of civilization" (whatever that is) or some other cause that cannot actually be measured. These causes demand more than a rational, measured support. One would do anything to win a war because the imagined stakes are so high. As a result, democracy and citizen involvement can actually work against proper restraint.

Yet democracy also increases room for restraint in some ways. Citizens may think of themselves as critics. When citizens criticize the wars of the government, they usually reawaken the just war criteria, which are relevant and speak to government.

The American experience

U.S. citizens used the just war criteria to criticize wars beginning with the War of 1812. Some dissenters said that it was not a just war, that the cause was not worth it, and that it was not a matter of last resort. The dissenters were outvoted.

The next major experience of that sort happened during the war against Mexico. Numerous American figures, including politicians like Abraham Lincoln (then in the minority) and nonpolitical figures like Henry David Thoreau, used just war categories to say that the United States had no grounds for what it was doing against Mexico.

Just war categories were forgotten when the United States stepped into World War I. That war became a crusade to be fought for the overarching cause of saving the world. It was not a soberly measured use of minimum necessary means to obtain a modest goal. In order to get us into the war (after he had run for president on the grounds of keeping us out), Woodrow Wilson made it a crusade rather than a just war.

Once that war ended, pacifists and soldiers alike condemned it using just war categories. The military elite of both sides did not think World War I should have been fought. The German high command actually told the Kaiser, "We think we can win it in six months, but if we cannot we should not try." The French high command told the Paris government the same thing. They were both wrong, of course. Military historians have had the honesty to admit that World War I should not have been fought. It was neither proportionate nor winnable in the scope of the resources available. It was not worth the stakes.

In our experience, it was only Vietnam that made those categories widely usable in the minds of ordinary citizens. *Just authority?* What business did the United States have being in Southeast Asia? Was the Saigon regime a legitimate regime?

Just means? We can say that the means were not just based on what we were told about the nondiscriminating use of weapons, free-fire zones, and the difficulty in telling who in a Vietnamese village was a soldier.

Last resort? Had we explored all other possible ways of obtaining whatever it was we were fighting for?

Good intention? Many in our country said that the purpose of the Vietnam adventure was not to save Vietnam but to save the whole world. The conflict was to keep the "domino effect" from bringing all Asia into the Communist camp. That is not a just intention if our real enemy (as they told us then) was Communist China or the Soviet Union.

The just war vocabulary seemed to be a good instrument for expressing dissent over the Vietnam experience. Most of the young men who refused to go were not pacifist in the thorough or radical sense. They did not think that all war was necessarily wrong but that Vietnam at least was wrong. They explained their position using the just war criteria.

Refusing to fight

We now move beyond the citizen as critic to the citizen as actively refusing to serve. This is not a new idea. Martin Luther had already said a soldier should accept martyrdom rather than serve in a war he knows is unjust. Luther also said, however, that an ordinary soldier probably does not know as much as his prince. The logical imperative of refusing to fight in an unjust war, which Luther affirmed, therefore became an empty mandate in Lutheran experience. Not only in Luther's time but ever since, the likelihood that one will have enough information to second guess the government is practically zero.

The concept of just war was enormously heightened in the set of political events surrounding the Nuremberg trials. After World War II, a series of trials was held in various places in Europe as well as the Pacific. The most dramatic institutionalization of the procedures was in the city of Nuremberg, where the allies set up a special court to convict certain Nazi leaders of war crimes. Those leaders were condemned for not having disobeyed an unjust order, that is, for failing to refuse to fight in an unjust war. The notion of conscientious refusal was tightened enormously because of these trials.

Historians and political scientists continue to debate whether the Nuremberg phenomenon was authentic—whether it was honest or whether it should be invalidated because it was a "victor's justice." At the very least, it acted out the claim that it is a moral and legal responsibility to refuse to participate in unjust military operations.

Because of Nuremberg, it became thinkable for Americans to say of Vietnam, "I cannot participate in that." Some Americans appealed directly to the Nuremberg precedent. Institutions in this country have continued to define the criteria of the limits of violence more carefully. Since the American Civil War, we have internal military codes. The American code was first drafted by the immigrant political scientist, Francis Lieber, at the request of Lincoln's government. It is natural that if a country is fighting a civil war, it will be concerned about which actions are proper and which are not because the killing is taking place among brothers. The Civil War saw the beginning of a series of internal military codes in which procedures for giving and obeying orders were themselves filtered through a set of limits. Those limits concerned what could be justified within the chain of command.

It is possible to refuse to obey an unjust order, although it is not easy to do, and it is not made easier by the mores of the military establishment. It is also possible in extreme cases to be prosecuted for not refusing to obey an unjust order or for committing an atrocity. Even if not often enforced, at least it is on the record that a person can be prosecuted for committing an atrocity. The mere existence of military law is itself an institutionalization of the just war tradition.

Could a war be just today?

Let us leap from our recent Vietnam experience to our current thought about war. The staff expert on limited war policies for the Roman Catholic bishops of the United States is Bryan Hehir. He said in an article in the Catholic opinion journal *Commonweal* last March that practically all serious theological ethicists categorically reject an all-out nuclear exchange. They differ, however, on where the lower end of that rejection comes. In other words, if you reject an all-out exchange, what would be the non-all-out exchange? Would you dismantle the machinery you already have? They differ on related issues about nuclear war, but there is nobody, says Hehir, in favor of the moral possibility of a nuclear war.

That is a summary of an enormous renewal of research and writing in the field of just war theory that has burgeoned in theological literature. Dissertations, history surveys, and contemporary debates have made the theme of the just war visible as it has not been for centuries. On the other hand, Hehir also reports that although the theological ethicists think the way they do, the Pentagon continues to believe that an atomic war is wageable.

In the face of all this history, we can return to various rephrasings of the original question. Does the tradition work? Has any past war met all the criteria? Met even most of the criteria? We can say at least that the major wars did not fulfill just war criteria. The Napoleonic wars did not, on either side. The Crimean War did not, on either side. The American Civil War did not, on either side. World War I did not, on either side.

Has any responsible statesperson in the past rejected a war on moral grounds that would have been otherwise politically attractive? Opposition politicians have— Abraham Lincoln rejected the American attack on Mexico. But has a politician in power ever used just war criteria to say of an attractive war (one that would put our country in a better position and would be good for our economy and prestige) that it should not be fought because it does not meet the rules?

More importantly, we should ask: *If* the theory were to be credible, how would we define the criteria so reliably that it would allow us to exercise restraint effectively? This would take more definition of what the criteria are and how they work. When you ask about proportionate damage, for instance, the whole war must do less destruction than what would happen if it was not fought. How do you measure that? How many freedoms are worth how many lives, how many buildings? How many lives are worth how many dollars? Are enemy lives worth the same as our lives? Are civilian lives worth the same as military lives? Does not the whole idea of "proportion" wrongly assume that diverse values can be quantified all on one scale?

People justify using the atom bomb on Hiroshima and Nagasaki on the basis that it was proportionately less costly. Many more people would have died in fighting the battle on the ground. But the lives that were taken in Hiroshima and Nagasaki were civilian, and the lives that would have been lost in invading Japan would have been military lives. Are those to be weighed one to one? Or is there some other way to calculate proportionality? All the people who use proportion language, which sounds mathematical, fail to spell out how you would actually do that weighing.

More important, the just war doctrine never tells us what to do if the criteria are not met. Do you go on fighting if your government tells you to? Or does it mean that everybody must become a conscientious objector? Does it mean that the other side wins?

Ralph Potter, a conservative interpreter of the tradition who teaches ethics at Harvard, says that all the criteria for a just war must be met or the war is immoral. Others would say that it is enough simply to have thought about those questions. They would say that the tradition provides a checklist of things not to forget, and if you cover most of them most of the time, that is about all that can be expected.

If the just war tradition were to be workable, people would have to learn in their catechetical instruction as Christians what those criteria are. The church would have to have resources to find the facts, because the just war approach is based on facts—unlike the anything-goes approach, the crusade approach, and the pacifist approach.

What is a just cause? What is at stake? Is it a matter of last resort? What did the enemy do? What is a righteous government? All those are questions of verifiable, empirical facts.

Do we trust the government's information or do we need our own information? If we are ever going to be able to dissent, we need our own sources of information. In the United States we do not have the instruments for our own information in many cases, although more freedom of speech exists here than in many parts of the world.

We also have to think about alternatives to fighting an unjust war. If we cannot fight the war, what else can we do? There should be contingency scenarios. If the government sees that a war is not justified, what is their alternative for maintaining the national dignity without a war? Government in exile? Underground government? Passive resistance? What would their instruments be? Are there think tanks planning alternatives?

If a government persists in waging a war that Christians or moral people know is unjustified, have those moral people thought ahead about their readiness for massive conscientious objection? That is a prerequisite for the credibility of a person claiming to hold to the just war tradition.

Thinking it through

We must make some other observations about the logic, especially about how it works in modern times. Just war logic assumes that somebody making the decisions is in control of the events. That was the case in medieval times. A prince could decide and he could know what he was deciding about. He knew how many soldiers it took to do what kind of damage. The chess game was fairly simple.

In modern times it is not simple. The potential for error or deception, for the loss of our communication instruments in a crucial situation, or for escalation through panic and the weight of irrational factors like national pride is much greater. Those factors are magnified by the size of the weapons. The whole stance on war-making assumes the ability of leaders to make rational decisions. Our recent experience in many parts of the world, Iran for instance, indicates that what we think is rational is not what somebody else may think is rational. Patterns of decision making do not have that kind of clarity.

The just war logic also assumes a certain amount of democratic honesty, such that a citizen can know what is being done in his or her name. Some of the contemporary theories assume at the same time that the citizens do not know, because otherwise the bluff would not hold—and deterrence is based on the bluff. You threaten to do something that you cannot do morally. For example, it would be wrong to use certain bombs, but it is not wrong to make people think you are going to use them. That means that you may have to fool *your* high command into thinking you have them ready to use, but still be able to say no when the crunch comes. That is a simple example of the new kinds of dilemmas that arise in an age of total war.

A medieval war could be winnable. In a modern war, winning is almost an impossible concept because of the amount of destruction that would occur through the exchange of weapons. Even if one side wound up having more weapons than the other side, even if one country's land was more destroyed than the others, has anyone really won? Certainly not in a total nuclear exchange.

In more ways than we have had time to look at, the phenomenon of modern war goes beyond the limits of the just war criteria. The evidence drives me to conclude that it is not factually true that most Christians think or act according to classical just war tradition. Most Christians have not been taught by their churches what the conditions of just war are. Most do not try to find independent sources of information.

Most do not make contingency plans in case disobedience becomes necessary. Rather, what people really live out is a mix of two other views.

People mix some measure of "realism" or Machiavellianism and simple patriotism or chauvinism. They assume that our government makes the right decisions and combine that belief with some measure of ideology— the crusade, the fight for freedom, or the transcendent cause in the face of which the adversary has no rights.

The theologians have proclaimed the intellectual integrity of the just war tradition. Those who have looked closely at the tradition, however, become increasingly critical. That is a point in favor of their moral honesty, although usually their criticism is done after the fact. Throughout the time we were in Vietnam, for instance, most just war thinkers were still asking about Hiroshima. Some politicians and military commanders are self-critical. Some take risks and jeopardize their offices by taking oppositional stances out of personal integrity.

When it is used, the just war tradition can operate for restraint. It is still the case that the just war type of reasoning is morally superior to the other available nonpacifist options. It does not say "anything goes." It does not say we are fighting for the glory of God. Both of those are worse options—and, regrettably, both are chosen by most people.

The only kind of war that any Christian or any non-Christian morally accountable person has any conceivable right to let happen, would be one that would meet those tests of intention, limited damage, proportionality, noncombatant immunity, last resort, etc.

The case for war must always have the burden of proof, and that burden of proof is getting harder and harder to deliver. Dialogue over whether there could ever be a war small enough, polite enough, indispensable enough, unavoidable enough to meet the criteria, and still be winnable, is a worthwhile intellectual exercise, but it is not our fundamental moral duty. Our duty is to stop fighting wars that *do not* meet just war criteria.

Part Three
Witness in Action

9

Self-Defense[1]

Christians committed to nonviolence meet no objection more frequently than the one that expresses itself in questions like, "But what would you do if someone attacked your family?" This is by far the most common reaction to an explanation of the Christian pacifist position toward self-defense and participation in war. This single question carries within it most of the diverse arguments that people raise about this topic. If we answer it adequately, then our position should be as secure as an argument can make it.

Not my will, but God's

There are several parts of our answer to such a question. Not all of the possible answers are equally forceful,

---

1. This chapter was originally published as "What Would You Do If . . . ? A Series," *The Youth's Christian Companion*, June 5, 1949, 595; June 12, 607; June 19, 615; June 26, 620; July 10, 636; July 17, 644–645; July 24, 637; Aug. 7, 668 (originally published under the pseudonym "Ein Wiedertäufer"). This chapter should not be confused with Yoder's introductory chapter to *What Would You Do? A Serious Answer to a Standard Question* (Scottdale, PA: Herald Press, 1983; expanded ed. 1992). Though these chapters answer the same questions and are quite compatible with each another, there is surprisingly little overlap.

profound, or final, but all of them can help us get back to the two questions that really matter: What is the will of God for the Christian? And will you do it?

We have to keep these questions in mind as we deal with this question. As desirable as it is to understand our faith and defend it in discussions, for Christians the argument is not the main thing. Whatever our position is, it is wrong unless it is an expression of the love of God. If trying to win an argument leads us to hate the arguer or if our debating is not reinforced by a loving life, then we have lost the truth, regardless of what happens in the debate. The final proof of our position is not that we can defend it but that, God helping, we can live it. As we do so, our lives will extend God's love in the world by destroying the causes and healing the effects of sin.

We will not try to find the answers we are looking for by quoting isolated proof texts. We will turn to the general principles of God's will for the world. If we begin with that attitude instead of seeking for a direct "Thou shalt not join the United States Army" or a "Thou shalt not defend thy family," then the whole question will begin to clear up. Nonresistance will come to be seen in relation to the entire gospel as one of the basic elements in a Christian philosophy of life. The fact of God's love in the world will begin to replace our interest in ready-made answers and our answers will be truer because they will grow out of the reality of who God is.

To begin, we should recognize that "What would you do?" is not really the right question. We are discussing a matter of right and wrong, not trying to predict my future behavior. What I might *happen* to do in an imaginary situation has no connection to what I or anyone else *should* do. I have to admit that since I am a weak human being, I often do what I should not. So what I *would* do is no guide to finding out what I *should* do.

How do I find out, then, what I should do? For the Christian, there is only one answer to that question: God's will is the only "should" in my life. That is the correct place to start. We may find God's will partly in our own minds and partly from experience in the world around us, but we can never find it completely except in Jesus. This means that we have to study the Bible to find our answer.

What Jesus says about self-defense is pretty clear: "But I say to you, Do not resist an evildoer. But if anyone strikes you on the right cheek, turn the other also; and if anyone wants to sue you and take your coat, give your cloak as well; and if anyone forces you to go one mile, go also the second mile. Love your enemies and pray for those who persecute you" (Matthew 5:39-41, 44). You ask whether I would defend my family. Here is the example of the most defense-worthy man who ever lived: "When those who were around him saw what was coming, they asked, 'Lord, should we strike with the sword?' Then one of them struck the slave of the high priest and cut off his right ear. But Jesus said, 'No more of this!' And he touched his ear and healed him" (Luke 22:49-51). Or again: "Do you think that I cannot appeal to my Father, and he will at once send me more than twelve legions of angels?" (Matthew 26:53).[2]

If Jesus demonstrated in his death such an attitude toward self-defense, and if his Father did nothing to interfere, then my attitude toward defending myself and my loved ones can be no different. Whatever I would do, it is clear from the example of God's own actions that I should do nothing that would be untrue to God's nature, to God's will for me, and to God's love working in me.

Eternal consequences

As a Christian, I should guide all my actions, including what I would do about someone attacking my family, by what I know about the moral importance of eternity. The

---

2. It is true that Jesus had to accept arrest and face the cross for the salvation of the world in a sense that his followers do not (although he made clear that we, too, must bear a cross). Yet we should not forget that how Jesus faced those who unjustly arrested him stands in line with his teaching about how his followers are supposed to deal with those who unjustly mistreat them (Matthew 5:38-48). We should also remember that Jesus used his response to his arrest as an opportunity to teach his disciples about right and wrong ways to respond to injustice. When Peter pulled out the sword and struck one of his opponents, Jesus said, "all who take the sword will perish by the sword" (Matthew 26:52). Jesus' arrest at Gethsemane is therefore both unique to Jesus and relevant to his followers.

really important world in which Christians live, the realm of obedience to God, is the area in which moral decisions must be made. This means that before settling this one question we must remind ourselves of the bigger truths it involves.

One such truth is that what we do in this life matters in eternity. Heaven and hell, depending on what the individual does about God's love, seem to some people to be old-fashioned ideas, but without understanding them we can never understand either God's goodness or our free will. If our choices are free, that means that we can choose to disobey God. If God is completely good, then that choice will separate us from God. And if anyone refuses to accept the invitation of Christ to end that separation by repentance, faith, and obedience, then that separation must continue. Such separation is the meaning of hell. In the same way, the Christian's eternal union with God, which begins even in this world, is also the result of accepting God's gift of forgiveness and faithfulness.

With this in mind, let us return to our original question. Assuming that I am Christian and the attackers are not, then what choices are open to me? I could do everything possible to stop them, even killing them if need be. But then I would be guilty of sin and violating the law of God's love. What is worse, by ending the attackers' life, I would condemn them to eternal death by robbing them of any opportunity for repentance. I would be guilty of destroying not only their bodily life, but also the life of their spirit. Or, on the other hand, I could show them the suffering, forgiving love of God that is possible in my life only because of Christ. I could try to reason with them and I might try to restrain them without injuring them, but if a life should have to be lost, it should be mine. If injuries should be incurred, I should bear them. Then my life, being lost, would be saved for an eternity with God. The attackers, meanwhile, would live. Perhaps they would repent, perhaps they would be stirred by my love—but whatever their fate, it would not have been sealed by my hand.

To put it simply, a part of my answer to the question we started with is simply to ask another question. Which is better, from the Christian point of view: for me to be sent to heaven, or to send someone else to hell?

Defining defense

Now let us think a little more carefully about the whole idea of defense. What is it, anyway? The term is used as if we all know what it means, but its meaning is often foggy in our minds.

To begin, let us say that "to defend" means to ward off danger and protect from harm. Simple enough, it seems. But the hidden question is what we mean by "harm" and "danger." "The harm or danger caused by the attacker, of course." But what is the harm the attacker can cause? Perhaps pain, material loss, or at most, loss of life. These are real dangers, of course, but there could be worse.

Here is where the Christian starts to answer the question of defense. Loss of life or property is not the greatest harm that can come to a Christian. By some people's standards, nothing is more valuable and no loss could be greater, but the Christian cares more about God's will. The true Christian has no higher purpose than to obey and fulfill that will. That is what makes one a Christian. The Christian is willing to take any loss, even life, if it is necessarily involved in our relation to God. The apostle Paul says, "I regard everything as loss because of the surpassing value of knowing Christ Jesus my Lord. For his sake I have suffered the loss of all things" (Philippians 3:8).

So the greatest harm that can come to Christians (or to anyone else, really, but only the Christian knows it fully) is for them to break the bond of faith and obedience that holds them to God. To preserve that bond and prevent that harm, our lives must be ruled by the love of God, which never returns evil for evil or prevents evil with evil. The love of God turns the other cheek, goes the second mile, and forgives seventy times seven times. That kind of love sometimes involves earthly losses. True Christians, to defend themselves from the greatest possible harm, willingly accept the risk of smaller losses. The best defense for Christians is absolute insistence on God's will, which means love and nonresistance.

You see by now what this does to our original question about defending my family or myself by force and by disobedience to the law of love. Any kind of hateful defense would be the worst harm I could inflict on myself. It would really be no defense at all, from the Christian standpoint. As for defending my family, they, too, are Christian. And since they want God's will to be done, they would not want me to sin and disobey that will to preserve their lives.

Love prevents a multitude of sins

As soon as the "What would you do?" question is asked, one important fact tends to slip out of the picture. We begin to assume that such a dangerous situation actually does exist, we attempt to decide how we would respond to the problem, and we almost forget that such a situation is an improbability. The whole question has a pretty big "if" in it, since in most people's lives such a danger never arises. The problem is imaginary, at least when it is asked.

Does this help answer the question? Certainly not. Even though hypothetical, the situation is not impossible and the Christian is not excused from seeking an answer. But the fact that the problem seldom comes up in a normal society shows us something that should not be forgotten.

It shows us that love can prevent problems as well as solve them. If I have done my part to see that something is done about the conditions in society and in people's minds that cause insanity, delinquency, or alcoholism, then it is much less likely that a maniac, criminal, or drunkard will ever endanger me or my family. If I am known throughout my community as a kind, helpful, and effective Christian, then I am much less likely to have to defend myself than if I regularly act out as a violent, vengeful person.

The same kind of thing can also be said of the problem a nation faces in war, although in that case the question is not solely an imaginary one. What if Hitler were about to occupy America? Well, for one thing, if the United States had done more to aid Germany in becoming a healthy, peaceful nation after World War I, there might have never been a Hitler. What about the Soviet Union? If other nations had done more to help her instead of fighting her for the first twenty years of her life; if the United States, England, and France had not invaded Russia to fight the Communists after World War I; if we had accepted her offer of universal disarmament in 1932; if we were not using the United Nations to isolate her politically; and if we were not threatening her with atom bombs; then who can say that the Soviet Union would be as dangerous a neighbor as it now is?

All of this should remind us of one principle that should apply in all our thinking. We must think of the future when we act in the present. What I do about today's problems is not only an effect of the problem and the cause that went before; it is also a cause that will begin a chain of further effects going on through time. If I commit an unloving act, the story does not end there. Its harmful results will help make the world worse to live in. But if I can, with God's help, act on the basis of God's love, then I have helped to make the world better and the results of that love do not handicap the people who follow me.

Although our war and self-defense might seem to be desirable when we concentrate on danger in the present, the picture changes when we look to the future. My participation in war cannot prevent war. It simply starts a chain of evil causes and effects that will lead to the next one. Only by breaking the chain of hatred with the power of love can I keep the problem from reoccurring.

So what would I do? I would meet the problem with the desire to bring no evil into the world. For I know that my own problem exists because I and others were not faithful enough to do good when we had the opportunity.

Violence and the Creator God

Christians must never lose sight of the fact that the God who tells us how to live is the God who made us and the world in which we live. That tells us something important about the Christian idea of goodness. What is good is not just the arbitrary desire of some ruler or legislature. It is actually a piece of information about how we, and the world, were made to work. Just as the manufacturer of a piece of machinery knows how it can be used most effectively, so the Creator of the universe and humanity knows best what sort of life we were meant for. No human philosopher has any more right to argue with God's revealed will than I would to tell the manufacturer of a camera that it can be best used as a machine gun.

So when the Creator of the world tells us that love should be the law of our lives, that information is more than just another piece of news. It should mean that my life is most effective, most useful, and most abundantly satisfying when love guides all my actions. Christians have been proving that ever since the time of Christ.

For one thing, love is "good psychology." There is no more effective way of dealing with other humans than to start by loving them. From the proverb that "A soft answer turns away wrath" (Proverbs 15:1) to the modern experts on how to win friends, it has always been evident that it is best to build life on the foundation of love.

Those who argue against nonresistance need to be reminded of this when constructing their "what if" scenario. They assume that a nonresistant reaction would always mean great loss, but that simply is not always true. Often, of course, the way of love is the way of the cross. But more often than we would generally predict, a loving response actually conquers evil.

Are the attackers insane? Calmness will be safer than violence. Are they looking for money? Give it to them. Are they hungry? Give them food and a job. Christian history is full of stories of resolved conflicts and defused dangers because of people who act lovingly to produce an outcome that violence never could have.

We must also remember that the use of force itself is not what Christians consider wrong. There is no rule that forbids the use of force in dealing with things in general. Killing trees for wood or animals for food is not prohibited. Restraint without injury may even be used by Christians dealing with the mentally ill or with children. Violence as a sin begins only when force is used with the intention of injury, coercion, or self-defense at the cost of others. We should also note that to seek sinful goals by other means, such as economic or psychological pressure, is just as sinful.

The truth is that Christians have available defenses—the power of love and the possibility of peaceful restraint—that will be more effective in most cases of human conflict than an attempt to injure an attacker. If not, we still have a clear answer in the law of love, which permits no exceptions. For what is the benefit of a law that is applied only when it is easy to obey?

> If you love those who love you, what credit is that to you? For even sinners love those who love them. If you do good to those who do good to you, what credit is that to you? For even sinners do the same. If you lend to those from whom you hope to receive, what credit is that to you? Even sinners lend to sinners, to receive as much again. But love your enemies, do good, and lend, expecting nothing in return. Your reward will be great, and you will be children of the Most High; for he is kind to the ungrateful and the wicked. Be merciful, just as your Father is merciful. (Luke 6:32-36)

"What would you do?" and war

People who carry on an argument by asking questions have to be reminded sometimes that a question is no proof of anything. The idea the question tries to prove is always one step further back. In the case of war, the thought goes something like this: (1) What would you do? (2) Of course, you would defend yourself by force. (3) Therefore, war is right.

So far, our time has been spent thinking about the step the asker takes between 1 and 2. That is the main question and should rightly be given our attention. But it is not the only question. The asker takes another step between 2 and 3, and that step deserves protest just as much as the first. Even if the answer in step 2 were right, war would still not be justified. While remembering where the main emphasis lies, let us go on as if we had agreed that defense would be justified.

First of all, there is a difference in the social significance of defense and war. If I protected my family against attack, I would be acting in the same way as a policeman who is preventing an action that would be forbidden by the law of the government over both of us. In war, that has never been true. There is no government that is superior to both parties in a war. There is no institution to order one nation to fight the other to prevent a crime. Nations on both sides of every war claim to be in the right and to be preventing crimes. Sometimes they even set up international courts or international governments to declare that the losers were wrong. Still, war is never fought because a righteous nation desires to prevent an action that is against the law of a higher government.

There is also a difference in the person who receives the injury. If I should use violence in defending myself, the only person injured would be the attacker. That is not true of modern war. Modern warfare does very little about the attackers. They are too heavily armed and fly too high and fast. In fact, modern warfare does little about defending one's loved ones. The main effort is to destroy the homeland of the enemy, including the homes, factories, and loved ones of the enemy. Such victims had little to do with supporting the attack and nothing to do with deciding on it. Modern war is a process of killing women, children, and the aged, while the attacker is safe somewhere behind armor, pushing buttons to murder still more innocent people. What would I do if . . . ? Well, for one thing, I would not fly to Russia to kill the attacker's spouse.

There is still one more objection to the logical jump from 2 to 3. We can see it easily in the world of an American politician who said something like, "We who believe in democracy and hold that violence is not the solution to human difficulties would disprove our own argument if we were to use violence ourselves to get our own way." The same thing applies in my personal situation. Attackers are doing something that is morally wrong; I am not. I am better than them and have the right to stop them with force, if necessary. But as soon as I have decided to use force, I have lowered myself to their level by using their methods. So I am no longer any better than them and have no right to stop them.

There is a proverb somewhere that says that those who begin to use their fists show that they have run out of arguments. We would say a similar thing about Christians who use non-Christian methods. They show that they have run out of love, and that means they have left Christ. For Christ never runs out of love, even when people crucify him.

Three final positions

Once more, let us look at the questioner's argument, instead of at the question. The questioner does not actually say where they stand on the issue, which makes it hard to know exactly what position we are responding to. In actuality there are at least three possible positions, if not more, held by Christians who take part in war. They all argue by asking this question, but for some of them it is not consistent and the Christian's answer should go behind that inconsistency.

The first position holds that defense by force is right for the Christian. People who believe this can logically ask "What would do you if . . . ?" This position is problematic because of biblical interpretation, the witness of Christian living, and the other reasons I have outlined here.

Many Christians take a different position. For them the question itself is illogical. For instance, there are many who consciously follow Martin Luther, who split Western Christianity in two by his theology. As a Christian, I should be nonresistant as the Bible directs. As a citizen, I must follow the government, not the Bible. In other words, war is wrong for the Christian, but right for the citizen for whom the government comes first.

The nonresistant answer here is obvious. The dilemma is described by Joshua, "Choose this day whom you will serve" (Joshua 24:15). The Christian's answer should also be the same as Joshua's. Jesus answered the same question when he instructed his followers to give "to Caesar the things that are Caesar's and to God the things that are God's" (Mark 12:17, RSV). Compared to what belongs to God, Caesar's share rightly is far less than half and can never include requiring disobedience to God or taking any part of life away from God's control.

There is one final position raised by some who agree that war is wrong. They argue that either it is the lesser of two evils or it is simply unavoidable (as in the case of a world war, for example). These positions are held by some very intelligent thinkers and can be very impressive. To answer them fully is not simple and cannot be done briefly, but the basis of the answer is abundantly clear. It became so as soon as they admitted that war is wrong. For no matter how impressive the argument may be for compromising with wrong, Jesus never compromised and that is the answer for us. Christians whose intention is discipleship have already made their decision about willingly doing what is wrong.

One final note about the "lesser-of-two-evils" argument. There are evils everywhere and there will be as long as this world stands. What the Christian seeks to avoid is not suffering evil, but committing evil. If we ask, "Which is worse, war or slavery?" perhaps to some minds slavery would be worse. But the question is, "Which is worse for me to do—kill or be a slave?" The answer is simple. The sin my enemies commit is not my first consideration. Loving them is.

10

Voting[1]

North American political culture, which is a comparatively solid crust of common language and rules of thumb, floats on a moving magma of unresolved debate between two contradictory views of the state. Because people begin from these differing but unstated definitions, they often end with divergent attitudes toward the moral meaning of elections.

The state as the center of history

The first view of the state has been common since the fourth century. In this view, Caesar is seen as God's primary instrument. If history moves in favorable ways, it is because Christian rulers find their regimes being blessed by peace and prosperity. If God sees fit to chastise, we see it in the infidel armies. Ever since the historian Eusebius and the theologian of history Augustine, the discernible movement of God's will

---

1. This chapter was originally published as "The National Ritual: Biblical Realism and the Elections," *Sojourners* (October 1976): 29–30. This article has been adjusted editorially to reflect the contexts of democracies like Canada's as well; the original was focused primarily on the U.S. context. Reprinted with permission from *Sojourners*, (800) 714-7474, www.sojo.net.

for the earthly city is carried by the civil authorities more than by the body of believers.

So one meaning of democracy in modern times is that this vision of sovereignty under God has been universalized. Renaissance, enlightenment, and the revolutions from 1689 to 1848 reshaped this view in numerous ways:

- The unit called "people" is now no longer Christendom or the Holy Roman Empire, but one "nation" defined in terms of dynasty, geography, language, bureaucracy, and a shared interpretation of their recent common history.
- The moral values represented by the "nation" need no longer be explicitly Christian, yet they have similar "religious" overtones and make similar claims to unify the nation/people in a morally transcendent cause ("liberty, equality, fraternity," or "blood and soil").
- It is argued that the advent of popular franchise has transferred to "the people" the attributes of the former king-by-divine-right. It had been said that the voice of the king was as the voice of God. But it is now the voice of the "people" that is the voice of God. Louis XIV had said of himself, "I am the State." That is now transferred to "the people." Yet this "people" can be perceived and can act only through a regime. Lincoln told the crowd at Gettysburg that that new reality was so integrally incarnate in his government that if the Union had lost the war against the South, "government of the people, by the people, and for the people" might have perished from the earth.

Thus for two centuries they have been telling us that we, the people, are governing ourselves, and we have believed it. Through our elected representatives, who speak for us, we translate into public policy our ideals and restrain one another's selfishness. If we do not like what they do in our name, we can get into the same arena to change things. It is both our privilege and our duty to do so. It follows that electoral events are the major landmarks in "the people's" history. Consequently, to work within this process, whether as candidate, party worker, or voter, is to discharge a near-divine civil mandate.

The activism and protest of the 1960s in the United States was still at home within this inherited idealism. The civil rights movement appealed to the egalitarian potential of the federal constitution against the racist laws of the states, and the "higher law" usually came through in the form of a Kennedy phone call. Even the more strident protest against Vietnam appealed to America's higher self-image. It is only meaningful to scold presidents for callousness or cheating if one holds them responsible to do the right.

It is helpful that the average Christian, especially the socially concerned believer, has discovered in recent times some of the cruder truths that political scientists and power brokers have known all along. But social science cannot explain the weight and urgency that most people place on the electoral process. It is not the case that most elections are crucial or that my vote matters much. So we must find the roots of this myth and rediscover the alternative.

The New Testament view of the state

The second view of the state is the only one that was conceivable for Christians in the first few centuries after Jesus. It is the explicit view of the New Testament, despite the efforts of scholars to drive a wedge between Jesus and Paul or between Revelation 13 and Romans 13. It is the only view that makes sense today for the vast majority of the world's population whose forms of government are moving not from the North Atlantic democratic heritage but from other pasts. It is the view that will increasingly make sense in the North Atlantic world as well, as our realism deepens and the vestiges of humanist idealism crumble.

The exercise of government is by nature oligarchical (power wielded by an elite minority) and domineering. Democracy differs from other forms of government in degree, not in kind. Democratic safeguards (such as constitutionality, free speech, and the separation of powers) lessen the oppressiveness. They also facilitate the replacement of one oligarchy by another with less violence than in other systems. But they do not fundamentally change the meaning of "lording" over others (Luke 22:25). When the myth of rule by the people combines with short elective terms to undercut continuity and foster demagoguery (manipulating the masses) and the spoils system (awarding jobs to people who help get you elected), some kinds of exploitation in democracy may even be worse than in other systems.

Jesus does not condemn the fact of "lording" as if it could cease to be. He is no anarchist. He does not promise that his coming, the presence of the church, or the evolution of democracy will change the meaning of ruling. Nor does he approve of this arrangement as providential, as the order of creation, or as divinely mandated, as Christians since Constantine have done. He speaks only empirically: "That's the way it is." Our decisions about whether to try to be lords in our turn—to believe in "popular sovereignty" as a divine mandate to us all—belong in the context of this realism about power. Jesus' decision to be a servant rather than a lord was made in view of this same realism.

The exercise of lordship always makes moral claims for itself. Jesus does not say that the rulers are benefactors but that they claim to be. They undergird their control with a scaffolding of moral justification. This is true not only of dictatorships, but also of democracies, in that the moral claims of the contenders in the power process (party identities, platforms, campaign promises, appeals to consensus backing) deepen the dialogue between rulers and ruled.

Within the realism about the power game that these words of Jesus reflect, we can be sober about the election process. The vote does not mean that we are governing ourselves. It is not true in most cases that concerned people's first duty is to push, in the party and at the polls, so that their particular minority view may poll just a bit stronger and will have a better chance of gaining ground four or eight years later. Christians in the North Atlantic world must develop a chastened relativism about democracy. If we do, it will save us both from scolding those under other regimes for not rebelling against their rulers and from pitying them.

A more biblical and realistic approach

Although the vote does not mean that we are ruling ourselves, we can rejoice that it does mean that the rulers regularly consult their subjects. A system in which the subjects are consulted and in which the oligarchy can be changed nonviolently is better than other systems. So we shall participate gratefully, though with low expectations, to the extent that real options are at stake.

Within these properly lowered expectations, we can be less tense about which side to take, for the criteria that guide us may be more varied. We need no longer assume that, as little Constantines, we must always decide on "the right." Other things being equal, we may vote for the weaker side in order to counteract the winner's margin of self-righteousness. We may vote for Nixon in 1960 on grounds that the country needs the humiliation to which his proud nationalism must lead. We may ask to be counted against the system by abstaining or by throwing away a vote in support for a hopeless cause like Prohibition or Dr. Spock.[2]

Each of these approaches seems irresponsible within the standard "of the people, by the people" myth. Yet each may be integrated into other nonelectoral forms of witness and conscientious discharge of local vocational duties. These include things like pilot enterprises with alternative solutions, occasional nonviolent obstruction, prophetic pastoring of honest persons in high places, lobbying for the unrepresented "widow and orphan," and molding public awareness through information.

We should remain open to the possibility of a single-issue vote where Christians across the nation ought to unite with one voice, but we should not expect this case to be frequent.

We should expect relatively better results, as witness and as power-for-change, from nonelectoral modes of presence than from the franchise. From this standpoint, voting is not a ritual affirmation of moral solidarity with the system, as both hippies and superpatriots would contend. Rather, it is one way, and one of the weaker and vaguer ways, to speak truth to power. We may do well to support this channel with

---

2. Dr. Spock, not to be confused with the *Star Trek* character, was a renowned pediatrician and author who spoke out against the Vietnam War. He was the People's Party candidate for the United States presidency in 1972. Yoder is likely referring to this election.

our low-key participation, since a regime where it functions is a lesser evil (all other things being equal) than one where it does not. We must remember, however, that our discharge of this civil duty will be more morally serious if we take it less seriously.

11

Veteran's Day[1]

This is the day that had been known for some time as Armistice Day. Forty-five years ago today saw the end of active hostilities in World War I, which had been fought at enormous cost and with the declared purpose of "ending all war." The celebration of the armistice was enormously joyful in the immediately following years because of the confidence of many who sincerely believed that this war *had* ended all war. Yet within ten years, it was clear that no problems had been solved. Certain nations would not join the League of Nations and there were difficulties in Europe. Within fifteen years Hitler was on his way. Within twenty years there was war in Europe. Within twenty-five years the world was at the peak of another conflict.

Now, in the United States, we speak instead of "Veteran's Day."[2] This involves a significant shift of meaning. When November 11 came to be a national holiday, the celebration was a testimony to the conviction that there should be no more war and a rejoicing that war had ended. Somehow the celebration of this holiday has come to mean almost the opposite. It now ratifies and legitimizes war as an institution.

---

1. This chapter was originally a sermon preached at Goshen College Chapel on Nov. 11, 1963.
2. Remembrance Day in Canada.

This has happened at the most inappropriate time. Americans were confident and optimistic after World War I because of the feeling that there was a clear purpose that gave meaning to victory. This feeling came back again at the end of the Second World War. This time the war had been fought "to make the world safe for democracy," admittedly a more modest aim.[3] Yet even measured by that aim, World War II has been a failure. Partly because of the way that war was fought, including the compromises and alliances made in order to win it, we cannot say that Poland or Czechoslovakia has a democratic government as it did in the 1930s. We cannot say that the future of democracy and civil liberties is assured in France and West Germany. Those nations which have become democracies since 1935, like India and Nigeria, have gained independence as democratic states without war. The powers of the antidemocratic governments in the world are stronger than they have ever been. What then is there to celebrate? Or what should we do if we cannot celebrate this day with its original meaning because of the history that has happened? With this question in mind, we turn to one of the writings of the apostles.

Prayer for rulers

First of all, then, I urge that supplications, prayers, intercessions, and thanksgivings be made for everyone, for kings and all who are in high positions, so that we may lead a quiet and peaceable life in all godliness and dignity. This is right and is acceptable in the sight of God our Savior, who desires everyone to be saved and to come to the knowledge of the truth. For there is one God; there is also one mediator between God and humankind, Christ Jesus, himself human, who gave himself a ransom for all—this was attested at the right time. For this I was appointed a herald and an apostle.

---

3. It is unclear why Yoder associated this slogan with World War II since Woodrow Wilson used it to justify American involvement in World War I. Yoder shows awareness of this fact in *Christian Attitudes to War, Peace, and Revolution* (Grand Rapids: Brazos Press, 2009), 215.

.., a teacher of the Gentiles in faith and truth. I desire, then, that in every place the men should pray, lifting up holy hands without anger or argument. (1 Timothy 2:1-8)

We see that the concern of the New Testament for those in high office was in the context of concern for *all people*. It was a prayerful concern for *all kings*. This means that Christian political loyalty is not a matter of preferring one sovereign to another or one political system to another, but rather loyalty to the principle that there shall be government.

Why should governments preserve "peace and tranquility"? So that Christians may go about their task of proclaiming to all that it is Christ Jesus who won freedom for all humanity. God has appointed that this should be proclaimed to the Gentiles (that is, the nations). This very phrase testifies that the Christian church knows no ethnic limitations and is not bound by any one national, cultural, or racial loyalty. Government exists in order to permit the church and the apostle to demonstrate and to proclaim the gospel. It is toward this end that we are called to pray for them.

The next thing we see about this prayer is that God's use of those in high office does not depend on what Christians do in the political realm. Rather, Christians pray for what God can do with Caesar as well as for the barbarian tribes to the north and south of the Roman Empire. Nor was this prayer concerned about whether governments are democratic or just. All that is asked for is the keeping of the peace. In that age, of course, the means of doing so were mostly totalitarian.

Faulty assumptions

This Christian vision of our attitude toward government poses a problem for most Christians today. Most North American Christians hold a view that contrasts with this apostolic view of the world. For North American Christians, it is obvious that half of the world is free and the other half is not. "Freedom" belongs to some people and not to others. To these people it is self-evident that "freedom" is *infinitely* valuable. If necessary they are willing to sacrifice anything else for it. In thinking about war, we often try to weigh and calculate one evil against another. If you had to decide between the "freedom" of the "free world" and the lives of one hundred million Soviet or Chinese citizens, then it is obvious that you will sacrifice the one hundred million lives. Even as the Department of Defense works to limit civilian casualties, the loophole stays open. Since freedom is infinitely valuable, we are willing to use nuclear weapons on whole cities "if we are driven to it."

A further assumption we have is that freedom is identical with national sovereignty. Freedom is not (as in the New Testament) really a matter of whether the church can go about doing its job with relative local liberty. Instead, the question is whether given nations are politically independent. It is clear to most people that the United States government is the guardian of the free world whether the rest of the free world wants to be guarded by the United States or not. It is likewise clear that the United States is wholly righteous. I recently heard a well-educated and influential individual state with great conviction that the United States has never attacked any country. He did not seem to be informed about the American occupation of parts of Soviet Russia between 1917 and 1920, the Spanish-American War, or the Mexican wars. He told us flatly that the American social order is an implementation of the Sermon on the Mount and the golden rule.

Lastly we often assume that everyone is to be measured by the same standards. For example, if the Soviet Union does not have as democratic a government as we, this difference calls for absolute condemnation. We fail to recognize that fifty years ago the Soviet Union was in the feudal age and that we have had centuries in which to work through the problems of figuring out what it means to be a relatively democratic society. Rather than measuring them by where they have come from, we measure them by where we are.

There is another way in which we expect everyone to be measured by the same standards. If there are halfway convincing reasons for a government to fight a war, it seems self-evident to some that it is not only permitted but in fact the duty of Christians to join in the war as well.

Our ultimate loyalty

My point in sketching this contrast between these two views—the biblical view of the state and the church and that which prevails in our society—is not to lead to any one pointed conclusion or to any extremely specific call to commitment. I simply want to remind us of the continued relevance of the task to which we have been called. This task is not celebrating the success of any military endeavor, but to be driven back to the one meaningful Christian starting point for thinking about these matters: prayerful subjection to the kings of this world and unlimited loyalty to the cause of a different kingdom.

Closing prayer

We pray, our Father, as we have been instructed, for all people. Break down the barriers of our concern that would limit our sympathy, loyalty, and awareness of need to our nation or to our half of the world. Teach us truly to bear in our hearts an awareness of your will that all people should come to the knowledge of truth. We pray, as we are instructed, for all sovereigns and those in high places. We pray for the governments of Western nations. We pray as well for the governments of Communist countries. We pray for the young democracies of Africa and southern Asia. We pray for those countries that are governed by dictators and military police. We pray for all those in high places and for those who contribute to making their decisions and to carrying them out. Grant through the outworking of all the selfishness and the idealism, the vision and the blindness of these people, that your will might be fulfilled that people might live together in peace. We pray not for the success or failure of any government's designs but for your providential guidance of all things toward the goals that you have fixed. We pray for your church, for Christians in relation to government. For those who are convinced that it is their calling to work within the making and implementing of policies of government, we ask that they might be stimulated to examine their calling and to let it be guided by your undiscriminating, loving, suffering concern for all people. For those who sense a conflict between their loyalty to government and their loyalty to you, to the church, and to all people, we ask you to clarify their vision and their determination to obey only you. For those who have no definite responsibility in the administration of this world, we pray that we might be protected from pharisaism, from self-righteousness, from thinking there is any virtue in being less involved than others, and from being unconcerned for decisions being made and injustices that happen. Hasten the day when every knee shall bow, in heaven, on earth, and under the earth, and every tongue confess, as we seek already to confess, that Jesus Christ is Lord, in whose name we pray, amen.

12

Conscientious Objection[1]

For those of us who are heirs of the Anabaptist-Mennonite tradition, it can almost appear as if the terms "peace testimony" and "conscientious objection" are clear, known, and firm positions that we merely hold without questioning. If that were so, we would simply proceed as though nonresistance is a predetermined and decided position and that we need only to justify it by collecting proof texts as the foundation for that view.

It is already clear from the gospel that this approach is impossible. For a Christian whose starting point is the gospel there can be no predetermined, decided issues before the Scriptures are consulted. Even the noblest tradition, one that is rich in the testimony of martyrs, is no adequate foundation for a position whose scriptural confirmation is sought only after it has already been decided upon. Faithfulness to our tradition requires in principle nothing else but that all traditions must be disregarded in order that the gospel alone stands as our starting point. The gospel itself should be the foundation and not the confirmation of our position.

---

1. This chapter was originally published as "The Peace Testimony and Conscientious Objection," trans. Horst Gerlach, *Gospel Herald*, Jan. 21, 1958.

These introductory comments are especially relevant in relation to peace testimony and conscientious objection. Sometimes we have turned our peace testimony into a groundless idealism. Sometimes we have turned conscientious objection into a heartless legalism. If we want to guard against the danger of distortion and misunderstanding, both now and in the future, we must first of all listen afresh to the gospel. Instead of looking for proof texts, we must pay attention to the whole testimony of the Scriptures. Only then will we be able to ask how much of our position is founded on the gospel.

The image of God

"See what love the Father has given us, that we should be called children of God" (1 John 3:1). The first page of the Bible proclaims the fundamental character of human life: God created humans "in the image of God" (Genesis 1:27). Humans share with no other creature this dignity and responsibility of being formed after God's own image. Theologians may debate what the term *image of God* means, but in context it is enough to know that what makes a human a human is found in likeness to the essence of God.

This likeness to the image of God also accompanies fallen humanity throughout history as a guarantee of the promised salvation. It is solemnly proclaimed to Noah that the lives of human beings are under divine protection because humans were made in God's image (Genesis 9:6). The fourth commandment expects humaneness of the Israelites because the God who brought Israel out of Egypt had acted "humanely." So it is stated, "Remember that you were a slave in the land of Egypt, and the Lord your God brought you out from there . . .therefore the Lord your God commanded you to keep the sabbath day" (Deuteronomy 5:15). The statement "You shall be holy for I the Lord your God am holy" (Leviticus 19:2) is the basis, the God-centered focus from which the individual demands of the old covenant received their significance. The commandment of the old covenant is not simply an arbitrary command to be nice. Rather, it is an offer of fellowship, an appeal to treat one's neighbors in a new way that corresponds to the nature of the gracious God of the covenant.

If the old covenant, which was incomplete and fragmentary, calls humanity to live according to the essence of God, this is much more clearly the case in the new: "Be perfect, therefore, as your heavenly Father is perfect" (Matthew 5:48). "But love your enemies, do good, and lend, expecting nothing in return. Your reward will be great, and you will be children of the Most High; for he is kind to the ungrateful and the wicked. Be merciful, just as your Father is merciful" (Luke 6:35-36). "As he is, so are we in this world" (1 John 4:17). We call God "our Father." We understand it as a sign of God's love that we have the privilege to be called "children of God." It is the fundamental principle of Christian obedience—or of Christian liberty, which is the same thing—that this parent-child relationship should be visible. We are chosen, predestined, called, and made righteous in order "to be conformed to the image of his Son, in order that he might be the firstborn within a large family" (Romans 8:29). God's purpose is that we all come "to the measure of the full stature of Christ" (Ephesians 4:13).

The God whom we image

But who is this God whom our nature and action should mirror? We could try to mold ourselves a God who would fit into our peace testimony as a projection of our idealism. As conscientious objectors, we could see God as an embodiment of our sense of responsibility. So we could, like the Greeks, look for wisdom, or like the Jews, for a sign (1 Corinthians 1:22). But that would not be the true God. The true God can only be found in one place, namely, where he first found us. The wisdom and the power of God are to be found in his message of Christ and in him crucified. The one who died on the cross was no wise Socrates, no exemplary legalist, no "teacher of righteousness" like the unknown man whom the Essenes revered. He was the only begotten Son in whom "the whole fullness of deity dwells bodily" (Colossians 2:9). It is the colossal claim of Christian belief that God was bodily present in a human being. It is this claim that makes discipleship our duty.

The God who is revealed in Christ is love. This is love that goes and seeks reconciliation with the enemy at one's own expense. This is love that even seeks to have fellowship with the unlovely and unwanted. This is love that gives up all claims to one's right, even one's own life, in order to give oneself completely to the other. When we were still the enemies of God, God showed love to us in that Christ died for us (Romans 5:8). God accomplished God's plan—fulfilling all righteousness and establishing the kingdom—only through total defeat. It pleased God to set even this crucified man as Messiah and Lord (Acts 2:36) because he became obedient even unto the death of the cross. Therefore, "God also highly exalted him and gave him the name that is above every name" (Philippians 2:9). This very "Lamb that was slaughtered" is worthy "to receive power and wealth and wisdom and might and honor and glory and blessing!" (Revelation 5:12).

If even God takes the way of suffering, so should we. If the God-man could and would not avoid suffering, then neither should we. If Jesus, as the true Messiah, paid with his life to establish God's kingdom, then his people should expect to follow him through this valley of the shadow of death.

Even if the Scriptures did not say a word on the subject, we would logically have to come to this conclusion. But we do not need to arrive logically at any conclusion. For scarcely anything is stated more clearly and impressively in the New Testament than this very thing. If the church is spoken of as the body of Christ, if it is said that the Holy Spirit is to dwell in it as a temple, then the conclusion is clear: the church's life is his life. Without Scripture, it would be blasphemous presumption to make such a claim for oneself or one's own group. But it is beyond a shadow of a doubt that the church of Christ, according to God's promise, has no choice but to accept this call to be called the children of God. This is no mere pious attitude. It is a relationship to the evil one and to evil, for the center of our discipleship lies in our participation in Christ's suffering love: "Whoever does not take up the cross and follow me is not worthy of me. Those who find their life will lose it, and those who lose their life for my sake will find it" (Matthew 10:38-39). "Servants are not greater than their master. If they persecuted me, they will persecute you" (John 15:20). Already in baptism the Christian has been "crucified with Christ," (Galatians 2:19), "in the likeness of his death" (Romans 6:5

KJV). The apostle Paul understood his labors as "becoming like him in his death" (Philippians 3:10) and as the completion of "what is lacking in Christ's afflictions" (Colossians 1:24). He was able to call his sufferings the "sufferings of Christ" (2 Corinthians 1:5) and to say that he was "always carrying in the body the death of Jesus, so that the life of Jesus may also be made visible in our bodies" (2 Corinthians 4:10). Here the apostle is not speaking only of himself: "For it has been granted to you on behalf of Christ not only to believe on him, but also to suffer for him . . . Have the same mindset as Christ Jesus, who . . . made himself nothing by taking the very nature of a servant . . . by becoming obedient to death" (Philippians 1:29; 2:5-8 NIV).

The call to discipleship

The church, living in true discipleship, devoted to its Lord in service and witness, loving and suffering for neighbor and stranger, friend and foe, will find no time for carnal warfare. This will not be out of legalism, whether derived from the sixth commandment or from the Sermon on the Mount. Rather, the church has other and higher purposes: "For our struggle is not against flesh and blood, but against the rulers, against the authorities, against the powers of this dark world and against the spiritual forces of evil in the heavenly realms" (Ephesians 6:12 NIV). If the church's ends are different from those of the world, then its means will also be different. The weapons we fight with are not the weapons of the world: "For the weapons of our warfare are not carnal but mighty in God" (2 Corinthians 10:4 KJV).

Thus our peace testimony and our conscientious objection to war are abundantly grounded in the very heart of the gospel. Our Anabaptist forebears found their way back to this understanding of the apostolic church with such clearness and consistency as has not come to light elsewhere in the history of the church. As Conrad Grebel wrote to Thomas Münzer in September, 1524, "Truly believing Christians are as sheep among wolves; sheep ready for slaughter. They must be baptized in fear and distress, affliction and death through which they are tested and attain the land of eternal rest, not by the destruction of physical enemies, but of spiritual ones. They need neither the worldly sword nor war, for they have abolished killing, or otherwise we would still be in the old covenant. . . . And even though you have to suffer for it, you should know that it cannot be any different. Christ has to suffer even more in his members. But he will strengthen them and keep them steadfast to the end."[2]

So today we should be able to write, "Christ has to suffer even more in his members. But he will strengthen them and keep them steadfast to the end." The foundation for our conscientious objection to war is the nonresistance of the one who "suffered for you, leaving you an example, so that you should follow in his steps. . . . When he was abused, he did not return abuse; when he suffered, he did not threaten" (1 Peter 2:21, 23). The foundations of our peace testimony are the work of the one who "came and proclaimed peace to you who were far off and peace to those who were near" (Ephesians 2:17).

Love and solidarity

This should settle the matter. But Christendom has given Christ's call for discipleship a different interpretation and therefore forces us to deal with one objection. Some say there is a special case that requires the Christian to take a different road. Sometimes it is necessary to defend the civil order. This order has to be preserved first, if necessary, by force. Because of Christians' solidarity with the human race, we cannot and should not withdraw from the sphere of this order. We have the same responsibility as all people, namely, first to protect order so that we may practice love.

We could say much in regard to this objection. I have already examined this question from the logical, philosophical, historical, and comparative religious points of view. The objection as well as the spirit of the age in which it has its roots are not at all convincing to many Christians. But here we want to ask only one question: What relation does this

---

2. The full context of this quote can be found in *The Sources of Swiss Anabaptism*, ed. Leland Harder (Scottdale, PA: Herald Press, 1985), 290.

objection have to the gospel of the cross of Christ? As soon as this question is raised the answer is obvious. The two are irreconcilable.

If it is true that order should precede love, Christ should have acted differently. First of all, he should have become the king of the Jews as was proposed to him several times. According to the New Testament this would have been possible. He should have established a just state order in the midst of the Jewish people. We should thank God throughout eternity for not doing this. Had God acted so, there would not have been a gospel. Jesus dismissed the idea that order should precede love as a devilish temptation.

Jesus knew about the solidarity of all people in their sinfulness. That is why he died for them. But he did not permit himself or his disciples to think that new moral responsibilities that deviate from the line of a suffering, loving discipleship should be deduced from this solidarity. "In every respect [Jesus] has been tested as we are, yet without sin" (Hebrews 4:15). If we share this confession of the epistle to the Hebrews, we confess that Jesus, who was truly and fully human, was not forced to take sinful action. On the contrary, it is especially through and because of his relation to the sinful solidarity of humanity that the obedience of Christ and his call to discipleship receive their ultimate seriousness.

This "peace testimony" is no "pacifism," as the term is used in political discussion today. It does not stand or fall with the possibility or predictability of political peace. It only has value because no political peace is possible or predictable. In a world where there are wars and rumors of wars, the church—whose citizenship is not of this world—calls believing Christians to love their neighbor in a way worthy of a disciple. Christians also call the unbelieving state, its unbelief notwithstanding, to righteousness and the preservation of peace.

Anyone can perform military service, but this service to the common good can only be performed by the church; anyone can preform a mu,itary service. The church knows that the Lord whom it serves and confesses and under whose cross it walks is also Lord of the state. The responsibility of the church to the world, our proper allegiance to the powers that be, is nothing other than discipleship: "I have set you an example, that you should also do as I have done to you. Very truly, I tell you, servants are not greater than their master, nor are messengers greater than the one who sent them. If you know these things, you are blessed if you do them" (John 13:15-17).

13

The Arms Race[1]

Among the various ways of ethical reasoning, two or three pre-
dominate. One is called "realistic" or "pragmatic." Some
call it a "morality of consequences" or "realism" or "responsibility." It assumes that we can and should take charge of
the course of events. We can and should weigh all of our
plans and values on a scale of more or less cost, more or less
benefit, more or less risk. Then we impose constraints on one
another to produce the best possible outcome.

If we differ with one another, it is about the core factors:
what weight we assign to the costs, risks, benefits, probabilities, and so on. Within that frame of reference, everyone
agrees that there is some point farther up the scale of costs or
farther down the scale of benefits where a war or a weapon
would be wrong. Yet we seldom agree on where that line
runs or whom we trust to calculate when we must stop.

The other mode of moral thought is sometimes called a
morality of principle or duty. This view is represented by the
slogan "let justice be done, even though the heavens fall."
Some deeds are always intrinsically wrong. Some duties are

---

1. This chapter was originally a talk given in Seattle on Sept.
25, 1982. John Howard Yoder Collection, Box 141, folder "Target
Seattle," Mennonite Church USA Archives, Goshen, Indiana.

always binding whatever the consequences. Then the choice is not one you measure on a scale with the middle range more interesting than the ends. It is a choice between day and night or between red and green.

When we talk about nuclear weapons, the debate is partly about which way of ethical reasoning fits our case. Are we quibbling over the fine tuning of debatable factors and contested probabilities? Are we in a world reasonable enough and controllable enough that the management model of moral decision can fit the case? Or is it a matter of global choice, holistic repentance, and hope?

If you watch closely, you will see each of these models at work in various positions. But we should not think that they correlate with specific views on the morality of nuclear arms. Obviously some pacifists talk of simple "principle." But so do some patriots. They say (without investing much imagination in putting themselves in the place of an Asian or a Central American) that they would rather be dead than "red." On the other side, some advocates of a so-called "strong defense posture" claim to be reasoning realistically, but so do their strongest critics.

Behind these two major models there is a third. It is more openly affirmed today than it used to be. It sets the self above other values. Instead of claiming to defend others by taking charge of the global system, even at some cost to oneself, now they say anyone has the right of self-affirmation and self-defense, even above others. You could draw an analogy with Adam Smith's view on the economy. He said that if we were all equally selfish but played according to the rules, then the economy would come out even (or better) in the end. Likewise, some claim that each person and community can be its own ultimate value and that each nation can be its own norm and judge. Then self-defense, even if it is at the cost of the rights of others, can be a right or even a duty. Once everyone sees themselves as potential victims, then everyone claims the right and duty to self-defense by whatever means necessary.

New technology and new political postures have coincided to produce a new awareness of the problem created by nuclear arms. Our society claims to operate by prudent calculation of self-interest and unselfish social management.

But this has pushed us to a paradoxical position: the only possible occasion for the use of maximum nuclear capability would be its failure to exercise its promised deterrent effect. At that point, it would be neither a prudent calculation nor an attempt to "manage" things. It would be revenge. So we should ask what other resources can lead us toward realistic commitment. Some of them will be specifically Christian, but most will have equivalents in other religions and moral systems.

A choice of neighbors

What is the human community that we want to defend and for which we are ready to run risks? Is it the nation? What are the moral claims of that unity today? Is it the political and military elite within a nation? It is that for many of us. But from a Christian perspective our neighbor must include the whole world. As David Brouwer puts it, "them is us over there." There is no moral ground for placing national identity above the rest of the world. There may be moral grounds for a constructive patriotism, but not at the cost of the others. That was the intent of the just war tradition, which states the limits of justifiable violence within the so-called "realistic" logic. War is regrettable, but it may have to be fought. If it is, it can be only for just causes, only under a legitimate authority, only as a last resort, only by limited and indispensable means, only with the right intention, only with respect for the immunity of the noncombatant, and so on.

The reason for this checklist is to remind even those who wield regrettably necessary force that the people on the other side are still persons. They still have moral rights, especially the population at large and third parties. Even the combatants have moral and legal rights. Historically, then, the just war theory is the pragmatic translation of the rights of the neighbor, including the enemy, which even the "realistic" perspective is committed to recognizing.

The Christian form of this is the call of Jesus to love our neighbor, including the enemy. I do not say "the command" of Jesus but "the call" because it is good news. It is a promise and a privilege. The good news is that you do not have to be boxed in by your definition of who you are. You do not have to be boxed in by the notion of enmity between you and someone else. That statement is not moral idealism; it is religious proclamation. Jesus offers us the privilege of loving our enemies in order that we may be like our Father in heaven. There are religious worldviews (including some that call themselves Christian) which do not believe that God is like that. There are nonreligious worldviews which do not believe that the world is like that. The world is not like that, most of the time, from some perspectives. But Jesus and his Father and Spirit are like that. That is what the cross of Christ means. That is why Christians speak of "good news." They announce that the mind behind the universe is biased in favor of reconciliation and pays the price for it. That is what Jesus' special concern for the underdog, the outsider, and the victim means.

The Christian reason for rejecting the arms race is not that it may escalate or lash back and endanger us. It is not that a Soviet missile pointed at Bangor or Chicago will spread its destruction where you or I live. It is that we have institutionalized the competition of world systems by placing millions of people "over there" in the category of "enemy." We are in bondage to the institutional commitment to call them enemies. That is wrong even if we do not plan to kill them. It was wrong to see them that way when they had no way to strike back and there was no danger of backlash or fallout. It was wrong in the European takeover of America when the original inhabitants of the continent were denied human dignity. It was wrong in the "good old days" when wars could be "won." It was wrong most fundamentally not because war gets out of hand, not because the other side is catching up with us, and not because of the waste or the risk of error. It is wrong religiously as a denial of the cross of Christ. Who is our neighbor? The God of Abraham, the God of all three Abrahamic faiths, calls believers into a wider vision and to a righteous compassion that reaches beyond themselves and for which they will sacrifice themselves. God calls them to recognize that they belong to a human community wider than clan or nation.

A choice of gods

Defined functionally, your god is what you sacrifice to and what you are ready to kill for. Your god is where you look to discern the direction of history. Your god is how you define human wholeness. You may define human wholeness by being ready to sacrifice for the drives of desire: that god is called "Eros." You may sacrifice for the urge to power: some call that "Prometheus." You may be giving up everything else for wealth: Jesus calls that "Mammon." Today we are talking especially about Mars, the god of war. These gods differ in shape and in the kind of sacrifices they demand. They differ in the aspect of human culture and creativity upon which they lay claim and in the need they seek to satisfy. They differ in the place they give to reason and in their attitude to culture. But deep down they are all the same. They all serve the self. They all lead you to make others the means to your ends. They turn people into objects or instruments, not actual persons. In our age, Mars is the most jealous and insatiable idol of all.

Long before Jesus, it was clearly said that there is but one God. We are told that this God is not to be represented by any image to which we should sacrifice anybody. Furthermore, there is no other God. If we take this seriously, it means that the nuclear challenge should not simply be seen as a threat to human dignity or survival but as a threat to authentic religion. The nuclear arms race is institutionalized idolatry. It is a consciously structured celebration of the readiness to make a burnt offering of one's fellow creatures for the sake of some other value. War has always done that. That fact is not a product of modernity. What modern technology has done is push this phenomenon to the point that the idolatry threatens not only a few specific enemies but whole nations—not only a few million contemporaries but the future of civilization. That changes everything and calls into question the three kinds of moral logic we began with.

A choice of hopes

The type of pragmatism that has brought us to where we are in the arms race is marked by a mood of despair. It constructs a worst-case scenario for what the Soviets are capable of doing. Against that it balances a best-case guess about how our systems will work, knowing all the while that its optimism is groundless. This brings us to the point where the best we can hope for is the forlorn hope of beating the odds in Russian roulette or the selfish hope that when the worst finally happens it will hit someone else.

The alternative to despair, for Christians, is repentance and resurrection. Call it creativity or serendipity if you prefer. To be human under God means the ever-renewed conviction that there can be another way. But simply plunging into what we think is the lesser of two evils will not help us find that other way. We will not find that other way if we refuse to listen to our critics, if we dehumanize our competitors, and if we authorize ourselves to hold hostage the unwilling subjects of opposing regimes. We may find that other way, however, if we accept the risks of mutual respect.

What our faith calls "hope" is not optimism. It is not founded in a fuzzy-minded trust that bureaucrats of right or left or middle will be fundamentally decent. It will put a little more trust, but not too much, in "the people" doing better. Real hope wagers on the priority of life over death—with or without what some would call "proof"—whatever the apparent odds. It finds that wager working wherever it has a chance. It finds that wager working in interpersonal reconciliation. It finds it working in creative problem solving. It finds it working in advocacy of nonviolent means of social change. To say this in specifically Christian terms, "if the Spirit of him who raised Jesus from the dead is living in you, he who raised Christ from the dead will also give life to your mortal bodies because of his Spirit who lives in you" (Romans 8:11). That is not poetry about some other world after we give up on this one. It is a statement of hope for *this* world.

A choice of selves

Our choice is a choice of identity. Who do we want to be? The old twisted dilemma about "red or dead" distorts the issue, but the issue is real. It could be that to renounce immoral weapons could cost us something, some privileges, perhaps some freedoms (though certainly our preparing to use immoral weapons does not help our freedoms much either). But the alternative is not to be dead, not to suffer death; it is to inflict death. In the worst-case scenario (and I do not grant that worst-case scenarios are fair) one choice is to be like Finland and the other is to be a nation of murderers. Is the latter who we want to be?

I said before that the dilemma between "pragmatism" and "principle" is not the best way to do ethics. We should remember that we seldom choose in a quandary between only two deeds or between two different cost/benefit tradeoffs. We choose between visions, scenarios, and stories. We choose what kind of character we want to be in what kind of story. If we do that, then we will not ask first what they want to do to us. We will ask whether we as a nation want to be the kind of nation that did that to them.

A moral shock wave would rumble through our culture if our self-righteousness was replaced with a real awareness of what we were already doing, who we are already preparing to be, and where we want to be in that story. It might be worse to win at any cost, to be undisputed king of a cadaver-strewn desert of our own making, than to lose. In sports we can afford to say that winning is all that matters. In real life there are other rules. You can win a fight and lose your soul. You can forfeit your reason for fighting.

Honesty and obedience

At the outset I left the old debate between the ethical types of reasoning—principle, prudence, and self-defense—lying there unresolved. After surveying the wider context we can now pick it up. The language of responsible calculation of lesser evils will say that if you see your duty as taking responsibility to defend endangered social values, then it must be within the restraints of the classical just war tradition. To be fair, that tradition has seldom been respected by political decision makers and seldom taught clearly by the churches. This would mean no all-out nuclear exchange and no counter-value strategy,[2] even in retaliation. If the just war tradition were being respected, we would be directing most

2. This type of military strategy targets the enemy's cities and civilian populations.

of our energy into constructive tasks and into more promising defensive strategies. Here is where the dishonesty shows. The "responsible" people have not been doing that. We say that our selfishness and our policing of the world is a last resort. The just war tradition says it has to be that. But it is not. It is our first line of defense. It has become an end in itself, against the honest pragmatism which would call for drawing lines short of present armament levels.

The language of absolute principle or simple obedience offers the privilege of loving the enemy. This may seem insufficient when standing alone in ethical theory, but it is still the best of the three kinds of logic. At least it shuts off some of the presumptuous scenarios that place a great deal of trust in the wisdom, information, and agency of a few nuclear button pushers somewhere.

The language of simple obedience will not be satisfied to declare the wrongness of killing. It drives us into the promises and duties of building a humane world. But we will not do that job of construction—which takes lead time, study, drudgery, discipline, and sacrifice—if we have one hand behind our back still holding the bomb we reserve the right to use. We cannot refloat the world economy if the world's reservoir of energy and intelligence is still being drained to make and deploy more arms that "must not be used" (at least according to those who argue the logic of nuclear deterrence).

None of the standard types of ethical reasoning give us one straight "how to do it" line that runs directly to a specific social strategy—whether this freeze or that, whether SALT[3] or START[4] as a first step or as a third step. Specific strategies and tactics are our problem most of the time. But those strategies and tactics are subject to the prior choice of who is our neighbor, who is our God, what we hope for, and our choice of the identity we want to live with and for. How to work out a new resolve to take God's world down another track, for both absolute and pragmatic reasons, will call for negotiation, reciprocity, and (relative) guarantees. But whether to make that first commitment does not. The

3. Strategic Arms Limitation Talks
4. Strategic Arms Reduction Treaty

decision to renounce idolatry, the decision to love the enemy, the decision to set out on a story worth living and dying for because we refuse to kill for it—that decision must be unilateral. The slogan is old but true: "There is no way to peace; peace is the way."[5]

---

5. This quote is attributed to A. J. Muste.

14

Income Tax[1]

As I grew into the earliest understandings of what it means to be a disciple of Jesus Christ in my late teens and early twenties, one of the deeply significant aspects of this discipleship that I sought to understand was what my teachers called nonresistance. I came to understand this word as pointing not to a social theory or a set of legal principles, but to one of the ways in which personal fellowship with Jesus Christ through his Spirit will normally work itself out in the life of the believer.

Nonresistance and the state in theory

Two things stood out in this understanding of discipleship in nonresistance, which came from my teachers and grew stronger in my own study and experience. First of all, to follow Christ on this path involved being enough different from the surrounding world to be considered unlikable or undesirable by certain powerful people and groups in the world. As a result of this opposition, the way of nonresistance may be called the way of the cross. It involves suffering. The

---

1. This chapter was originally published as "Why I Don't Pay All My Income Tax," *Gospel Herald* (January 22, 1963): 82, 91.

acceptance of such suffering is the test of the disciple's sincerity and faithfulness to Christ.

Second, the position of nonresistance should be a witness. The world operates through the interplay of selfishness against selfishness and violence against violence. A witness should show the world that this way of operating is subject to the condemnation of God and destined, even in this age, for ultimate judgment.

One other thing my teachers told me was that, according to God's will, the assignment of civil government is to keep the peace. The apostle Paul instructs Christians to offer "petitions, prayers, intercession and thanksgiving . . . for all people—for kings and all those in authority, that we may live peaceful and quiet lives in all godliness and holiness" (1 Timothy 2:1-2). Obviously we pray for "peaceful and quiet lives" not because we wish to be left alone but in order that the church may carry on its ministry, so that all people may find salvation and "come to the knowledge of the truth" (1 Timothy 2:4). The church's task is to bring people to know the truth. The state's task is to keep disorder to a minimum and maintain peace.

Now when I went out into life with these convictions, holding them sincerely as I had been taught, deepening them in my own study and experience, and sometimes even finding opportunities to share them with other Christians, I was increasingly struck by the fact that there was precious little in my own experience or that of the church that corresponded to this description of the state's task.

Nonresistance and the state in reality

The governments under which I lived, including the one whose passport I carried when I went overseas, were making a major contribution to the terror that threatens all nations of the world. They were taking the greatest initiative in poisoning the outer atmosphere of the globe and the inmost springs of heredity with nuclear tests. Statesmen were making their bids for election primarily on the basis of how "firm" they were prepared to be in threatening the other half of the world with nuclear destruction.

Christians and non-Christians alike in other parts of the world asked me what testimony was being given in America by nonresistant Christians, and at the cost of what suffering, in order to proclaim God's judgment upon the development of weapons that can be used only to break and not to defend the peace. Many are convicted that we cannot simply refuse military service and render some other useful service to society in its place. The position of the conscientious objector may be right for the young man to whom it applies. But the military authorities in Western nations have found a convenient way of putting such objectors into inconspicuous alternative service. If we want the Christian testimony against war to be adequate, we must do more. Alternative service says clearly that Christians cannot wage war and that we desire to serve our fellow humans in a useful way. But it does not say that the task of the state is to make peace. For most nonresistant Christians, conscientious objection and alternative civilian service involve no suffering and little sacrifice.

My testimony and taxes

These were my thoughts when I was reminded that there is one point at which almost every citizen does make a yearly contribution to the moral and financial support of the military monster. This gesture of support is carried out each spring when almost all wage earners give a share of their earnings to the federal government, more than half of which will *not* be used to keep the peace.

For a number of years, I had no chance to exercise responsibility over this use of my income, since my employer withheld the amount involved from my earnings. The spring of 1962 was the first time it fell to my personal responsibility and initiative to forward to the IRS an additional amount, going beyond what had been withheld. This additional amount due was significantly less than the proportion of my total taxes which I knew were being used for nonpeaceful purposes.

I therefore submitted to the director of internal revenue a full and conscientious report of my income, but wrote that I could not take the moral responsibility of forwarding to his government funds that I knew would be used for a purpose contrary to what government is supposed to be serving. I told him that I had no intention of profiting personally from my "tax objection." I was therefore forwarding an equivalent payment to Mennonite Central Committee for use in overseas war sufferers' relief.

In the course of time, I received an answer to this letter in the form of a conversation with a local IRS inspector. In a very polite way he informed me that he could not consider this as acceptable in lieu of payment to the director of internal revenue. He therefore drew from my bank account the amount which I had not forwarded in the routine way.

This much is my story. I want to clarify what I did and what it meant so that no one will misinterpret my actions.

Why refuse to pay taxes?

The point is not to keep the government from getting the money. Not only would this be legally impossible but it would be disobedient to Scripture. The New Testament is clear that the Christian will respond to any kind of coercion, legal or illegal, by giving not only his shirt but also his coat (Matthew 5:40). Once it was clear that the IRS inspector was disposed to take upon himself the responsibility of forcefully collecting the funds, as a "second mile" gesture I told him where he could find the money with the least difficulty.

The idea is not to avoid involvement in the evils of this fallen world or to "keep my hands clean" morally. No one avoids involvement in one form or another, and I would not be avoiding it if I had no taxes to pay. My concern is not to be morally immaculate by making absolutely no contribution to the war effort, but to give a testimony to government concerning its own obligation before God.

This is not tax evasion. I filed at the proper time a full and conscientiously accurate report on my income, and when further information came to light I amended my report accordingly. There is no intention to defraud and no liability to criminal prosecution.

This is not obstructionism. Numerous Christian and non-Christian "pacifists" express their disapproval of militarism by such symbolic gestures as illegally entering a missile base, sailing a boat into a restricted part of the Pacific just before bomb tests, or in other ways seeking dramatically to catch the attention of the public or of government administrators with their objection.

The action I am describing here differs from theirs in a number of ways. In the first place, I made clear, not only in my letter to the director of internal revenue but also in my conversation with the local inspector, that I now have and wish to maintain a healthy respect for the legitimate functions of government and for the persons who carry them out. I do not express my objection by getting in the way of some military sentinel or civilian truck driver whom I thus put in the embarrassing position of either being disobedient to his superiors or harming me, nor by becoming a problem for some judge who has no choice but to apply the law. I witness rather by writing and talking calmly to responsible civil servants who are my most direct contact with the process of government.

The only cost of this witness was paid in the form of a gift for relief. The actual amount of tax collected was increased by only a few cents' interest covering the time elapsed between April 15 and the date of collection. If the equivalent amount I had given for relief had been accepted by IRS in lieu of tax payment, I would have considered it as such in next year's reporting. However, since that payment was not accepted, I shall report it as a deductible contribution.

The way present tax laws operate, this approach (giving relief contributions in lieu of taxes) would cost the most to those who are most able to bear it because of their greater income. In contrast, the brunt of the sacrifice involved in being a conscientious objector in time of war is laid upon teenagers who are not chosen with a view to their being most qualified to bear it. If actions like my own were taken by a significant number of mature Mennonite wage earners, it would be the first time in our nation's history that the testimony to nonresistance was given primarily through the initiative of and at a cost to the most mature and responsible people in the church.

The New Testament and taxes

One question remains, which both the IRS inspector and my fellow Christians have already asked: *Does not the New Testament instruct us to pay our taxes?* Certainly it does and I want to pay my taxes and do pay them willingly as far as the functions of the United States government resemble what Jesus, Paul, and Peter were talking about. The New Testament teaches that Christians should be subject to political authority because, in the providence of God, the function of these authorities is to maintain peace. This is what I, in accordance with the instructions of the New Testament, am asking the American government to do.

In fact, I am willing to pay even when there is waste and fraud and incompetence, as well as for "welfare" services that go beyond what Jesus and the apostles had in mind. But I am not prepared to support voluntarily something that Jesus and Paul did not have in mind because it did not exist in the time of the New Testament. The authority that Jesus and Paul recognized was an authority within a given empire, an authority that—in spite of the violence, corruption, and fraudulent procedures of its tax collectors—did effectively maintain peace within the entire known world in New Testament times. The government of Rome was not spending more than half of its resources on preparations to destroy the rest of the world.

We know very little about significant political powers outside the Roman Empire. But we can say with certainty that there were no such powers, in any way comparable in importance to Rome itself, which Rome was preparing to destroy. The command to pay taxes in the New Testament is not a blanket command that we can simply obey without thinking. We cannot ignore the question of when paying taxes is giving to Caesar "the things that are Caesar's" and when what Caesar asks for (even taxes) is not his rightful due.

It is not my purpose to "agitate" for others to follow my example. I am rather asking counsel from my fellow Christians concerning the way I have been led. At the same time I am asking whether others have found more appropriate ways to render a worthwhile testimony against their nation's trust in the sword.

15

Civil Religion[1]

"We live in the flesh of course, but the muscles we fight
with are not flesh. Our war is not fought with weapons
of flesh, yet they are strong enough, in God's cause, to
demolish fortresses. We demolish sophistries, and the
arrogance that tries to resist the knowledge of God;
every thought is our prisoner, captured and brought
into obedience to Christ." (2 Corinthians 10:3-5 JB)

Many Christians have felt uneasy with how much battle language there is in the Bible. Sometimes it seems that the reason for that was the ethical issue of violence and war. But that does not explain it. There is just as much battle language in the New Testament where its meaning has nothing to do with taking life.

Paul's imagery here expresses that reality is a conflict. Something big is really at stake. Something big could be lost. Something big could be gained. We do not like conflict, so we try to tame the world. We try to make it less threatening,

---

1. This chapter was originally a sermon given the day before Memorial Day, June 3, 1984, at College Mennonite Church in Goshen, Indiana. The original audio is available at the MCUSA Archives in Goshen, Indiana. This audio was previously misplaced in a random box, but found in October 2011.

even if at the same time that also makes it less promising. We would like to have less to lose, even if that means there would be less to gain.

We are guided by visions of normalcy. We do not want the future too open. The mother assures the child that every-thing will be alright. The bureaucrat or business consultant defines a standard operating procedure so that no one will be surprised and nothing will be forgotten. Politicians promise people that they will restore traditional values: there will be prayer in the schools and jobs will be saved. We support the notion that there exists something like normalcy, that it existed in the past, that it can be restored, and that it would be good to restore it. We think that this restoration is what God is about. God is the one who sets things right. When "God's in His heaven—all's right with the world."[2]

The God and world of civil religion

In the classical days of European theater—from Euripides to the French Revolution—God used to be a character in the play. They called this character *deus ex machina* because God came down from heaven on a rope—out of the *machina*, the machinery back behind the curtain. God set things right by decreeing that somebody was not dead after all or that some-one was free from prison or that the plot that the author had not been able to untangle would come out right anyway. What God did was to set things right omnipotently and with-out any resistance. God was being all-powerful, all-wise, and all-seeing—like the parent we like our three-year-old children to think that we are.

But it is not that way in the Bible. The Lord of hosts is embattled. God wins most of the battles, but often at great cost. Sometimes the Lord loses because the people are unfaith-ful or unwise or because God's enemies are strong or shrewd. The Lord is reported to have created the universe but that does not mean that all things are divinely controlled. The universe soon got out of hand and is still out of hand. In the biblical vision, the happy hopefulness of Browning's famous verse from which I quoted—"God's in His heaven—all's

---

2. This is a reference to Robert Browning's poem *Pippa Passes*.

right with the world"—has been left behind long ago.

> The year doesn't stay at the spring,
> the day doesn't stay at the morn,
> the morning doesn't stay at seven,
> the hill-side doesn't stay dew-pearled,
> and the lark does not stay on the wing.[3]

God is not so much like the clockmaker whose master-piece just stands there beautifully crafted, intricate, and ticking correctly. God is rather like the sorcerer's apprentice, like Frankenstein, or an Oppenheimer, whose creature is out of control. God is not like the parent of a three-year-old, but like the parent of an adolescent or a young adult. Such a parent faces primarily the test of how to accept their offspring's rejection of their wisdom as well as their control.

The contrast between God the all-powerful, all-competent parent and God the embattled partisan runs all through our culture. We see it in the social sciences in a debate between balance models and conflict models. One set of social sciences sees the world as a system that sometimes gets out of balance. When there is such disequilibrium there has to be change to get it straight again. Balance or "homeostasis" is the dominant image, even though it is never perfectly achieved. Similarly some schools of psychology and mental health see the individual organism engaged in the process of seeing things whole, making sense of the world, and achieving coherence. When the world will not hang together for someone, we call that mental illness.

Balance and normalcy are also the vision behind many standard religious understandings and ceremonies. Religion celebrates the natural cycle of things: fertility in the spring (around Easter time), harvest in the fall, and solstice in midwinter (converging with Christmas). Or it celebrates the life-cycle of people: birth (which some celebrate with baptism), young adulthood (which others celebrate with baptism), graduation, marriage, anniversaries of all those things, and death. In this view of things, *God* is the word we

---

3. This is a reference to Browning's lines: "The year's at the spring, And day's at the morn; Morning's at seven; The hill-side's dew-pearled; The lark's on the wing." See *Pippa Passes*, 192.

use for the power behind our hope that the world will hold together for us.

What does that have to do with the Christian response to Memorial Day? Herbert Richardson once said that "the basic cultic rite of civil religion is human sacrifice in warfare" and that "the major holidays of the state are remembrances of great battles and its valorous dead."[4] Just this week our media reported the drama of thousands of people per day visiting the black granite wall in Washington where the names of some Vietnam War dead—only those on our side—stand inscribed. We saw on our televisions the pain of mothers, widows, and old buddies looking up the names of their loved ones. They reassured themselves that although the cause was unjust, although the tactical, strategic, and political thinking behind that war were clumsy and sometimes stupid, although the means were immoral, and although the war was lost, still somehow their loved one died for freedom. Somehow their personal tragedy is swallowed up in a larger whole because God has to be in his heaven.

The Christian response to civil religion

Since Memorial Day is the high holy day of American civil religion, Christians have to respond to it as such. My testimony this morning is that we are kept from being grasped by the biblical witness about God's peacemaking battle with rebellious creation because we have been hearing it through the filter of harmony thinking.

Paul has just said, "We are engaged in a battle. Our weapons are not carnal, but they are mighty. Its enemies are not flesh and blood, but cosmic powers" (1 Corinthians 10:3-5). The sixteenth century Radical Reformers believed that. Their resistance to state control, their readiness to suffer, their missionary mobility, and their trust in the New Testament as a field manual for the good fight of the faith put nonresistance and peaceableness in a context of combat and victory. They believed that as they loved their enemies and

---

4. Herbert Richardson, "Civil Religion in Theological Perspective," in *American Civil Religion* (New York: Harper & Row, 1974), 174.

died at the hands of their enemies, they were helping God win back the world. The Friends in the seventeenth century spoke of their movement as "The Lamb's War." Jesus had said to Peter that the gates of hell would not prevail against the church. Gates are the weak point of the fortification of any fortress. Hell is being attacked. Hell is on the defensive, not the church. The Lamb is winning by suffering. Great things are at stake. There can be genuine tragedy. God can be defeated for a time and at a place. But there can also be victorious reconciliation.

Over fifteen years ago I led the congregation in this place in singing a hymn by James Montgomery. He has many hymns in our hymnal, but not this one. It combines the imagery of a victorious procession from Psalm 24 with images from the book of Isaiah about gates of brass and iron from which God liberates people. Consider just a few of its verses:

> A holy war those servants wage;
> in that mysterious strife,
> the powers of heaven and hell engage
> for more than death or life.
> . . .
> Though few and small and weak your bands,
> strong in your Captain's strength
> go to the conquest of all lands;
> all must be his at length.
> . . .
> Then fear not, faint not, halt not now;
> quit you like men, be strong!
> To Christ shall all the nations bow,
> and sing with you this song.[5]

New forms of civil religion

The early Anabaptists and Quakers had a battle vision of the world. Somehow the climate has changed. This change keeps us from hearing the overtones of the witness of our ancestors. We have been taught to choose models of balance, ways the world is all right. There are three ways we have learned to think:

---

5. From the hymn "Lift Up Your Heads, Ye Gates of Brass."

1. There is the civil religion of Christendom, which was initiated at the beginning of the Middle Ages by the emperor Constantine. Today this is represented by Christian America. Nobody claims that this Christian social unity is perfect. There are flaws and flukes, but it is basically all right. There are also dangers and enemies, but most of them are foreign. God is in control. Basically we have it made. The Constantinian conservative says, "Let's keep it that way."

2. There is also a more left-leaning civil religion. This exhibits the same confidence, but on behalf of another cause. It is not the conservatism of Coolidge, Hoover, and Reagan, but the progressive spirit of Roosevelt, Kennedy, and Martin Luther King. We see America as less than complete and we want it to be more generous. But it would be basically still God's world. We look to liberation as a goal rather than freedom as a possession to be defended. But the vehicle of God's cause is still our national community and its power structures.

3. The third model of civil religion, which stands between Christendom on the right and Christendom on the left, envisions two forces in symbiosis. *Symbiosis* is the word in the realm of biology when two very different species live together, need each other, depend on one another, and keep each other alive. So we think of two realms interlocking. Martin Luther did it one way: with the religious realm under the gospel, the civic realm under the law, and both of them with the same citizens. Jews since the Middle Ages and migrant Mennonites since the seventeenth century do it another way: two groups that get along well. The small group is somewhat separate, somewhat withdrawn, and somewhat self-sufficient as a subcommunity that gets along well with a friendly government. We can afford to be nonresistant because our rulers are not friendly toward their enemies, but they are friendly toward us.

This symbiotic dualism has done much mischief in various ways, but the primary problem is that it keeps us from hearing the strand of conflict in the gospel. We heard the language of the New Testament or of our martyr ancestors as describing not a battle but a stable order of things. We used the language of nonconformity, but its tone and its tools were defensive. We used the language of mission, but it came to mean fishing people one by one out of the world, rather than gaining ground for God. We echoed their language of two kingdoms, but for us it meant two realms at peace with one another, with open borders like the United States and Canada. It did not mean heated battle between God's kingdom and Satan's.

As Mennonites in the last half-century moved from the country to the city, there has been considerable stirring around of rhetoric. People whose parents were dualists prefer to be more affirmative and more responsible. People whose parents were patriotic on the right become patriotic on the left. But all of this stirring around is within the same ground rules. It follows the same logic. The theme is still how to be on the winning side in a world that is fundamentally acceptable.

Thus, our pacifism is passive. We need not challenge or control the world because someone else does. The world is not rebellious and needing to be brought to its knees. It is only distorted and needing to be shored up or patched up.

Beyond the language of civil religion

Paul says his power is verbal and reasonable. In 2 Corinthians 10:4, he pits it against "sophistry" (in the JB or NEB) or "argument" (as in the NRSV and NIV). The clash is on the level of meaning and interpretation, words and values. It matters how you think. It matters which words you use.

Our peace commitment depends on using the right words. Some say our peace commitment is not relevant and others say it is not credible. Some say it is too simple and others say it is too complicated. Some say it is too demanding and others that it is not costly enough. The reason for all of this dismay and discussion is not primarily substantive. In other words, it is not that we have new facts that were not there before. The meaning of violence has not changed that much. The meaning of Jesus has not changed. What has changed is our words. People use words like "responsible," "involved," "liberation," and this creates uncertainty about which side of the issue we are on.

We live in an age when words are cheap and malleable. We have so many of them. We use them to make a sales pitch and to put the best possible spin on our intentions. Precisely for that reason, we often mistrust words.

Paul says that our thoughts can be taken captive in obedience to Jesus Christ (2 Corinthians 10:5). It does make a difference whether we say "nonresistance" or "nonviolence," whether we affirm "the sacredness of life" or "love of the enemy," whether a word like "responsibility," "involvement," or "power" has one meaning rather than another. It does matter whether we say "man" or "person."

Paul tells us that the lordship of Jesus Christ calls us to subject our language and our logic to him. If there is some argument, some sophistry, some social science axiom, some psychological wisdom, some lesson of history that says Jesus Christ cannot be Lord or that the cross cannot be God's power to save, then Paul would say there still is a battle. It is not Jesus who must yield.

Last week someone spoke about selective perception. That is, not seeing everything because of where you stand, or seeing it from only one vantage point. Our trouble is worse than that. It is more like distorting lenses or a mirror whose images are clear but right has become left. Naming the distortion is itself part of the battle.

A nation that tolerates Christians but increases its readiness to destroy others is no less ungodly than those who persecuted our forefathers. But we will find it harder to be critical of it. An economic system that rewards us but in which the bottom half of our society and the bottom 90 percent of the world is worse off this year than last is not "progress." This is so even if several million computers can talk to each other faster than ever before and even if the domestic employment picture is improving. The fact that we would be worse off if we lived somewhere else does not make North America less of a fallen world. We should measure a social order not by how it treats us but by how it treats the people on the bottom.

Reengaging God's battle

Paul is saying, "Our war is not fought with weapons of flesh, yet they are strong enough in God's cause to demolish fortresses. We demolish sophistries, and the arrogance that tries to resist the knowledge of God." *War* is still the word for that. There is a clash that refuses all peaceful symbiosis. That has not been changed by the conversion of Constantine, by the separation of church and state, by religious liberty, by the access of Jews or Christians to public office or to professional advancement. This clash or war is not destined to lose its character in the melting pot. That is the bad news.

But Paul has good news. He claims that his position is powerful. It is not weakness. It is not passivity. It may appear weak. It may be vulnerable in terms of what he calls "flesh." But it is not simple defeat. It is not senseless suffering. It is the victory that began at the cross, reached into the ordinary social realities of Mediterranean cities like Corinth, reconciled people with one another, and made them generous, inventive, and courageous. He had just described that reconciliation in 2 Corinthians 5:16-19. Ethnic standards have ceased to count in our awareness of a person. A new kind of society is building in which it does not matter from what group of people you come. He had just described generosity in chapter 8, talking about the Christians in Macedonia. They gave not only what they could afford, but far more. They gave first their own selves to God and then to others.

There is a sense of battle, but Paul is not besieged. He is not embattled; he thinks he is winning. He really believes that the resurrection of Jesus Christ was the hinge of history. The turning point was behind him. After the resurrection, for Paul, it is a downhill run.

Forty years ago this week the decisive event of World War II took place. They called it "D-Day." Once the Allied landing in Normandy was successful, the outcome of the war was decided. The surrender of Germany was almost a year away and many more casualties away, but it was sure (and if Hitler had not been crazy it would have come sooner). Soon after the war, the French theologian Oscar Cullman picked up that D-Day imagery to describe the apostle Paul's view of history.[6] The war is over in principle, but the continent must still be regained one mile at a time. Human history from the ascension to the end of time is like those eleven months at the end of World War II. That is only one figure of speech; there are others. But if we want to understand what Paul means by his battle imagery, it helps to know that for him the war was won. Christ's lordship was already established.

Why do we lack the same joyful sense of participation in victory? Why do we lack the same confidence that the building of the people of God is where the action is? Why do we avoid risk as if we feared that God's cause might lose? Maybe the reason is not that we have left the farm but the mentality with which we have gone to town. Maybe we have not been surprised by reconciliation the way Paul was. Maybe ethnic standards do count in our awareness of persons. Maybe we do credit our reputation for generosity more to the moral qualities of our kind of people, to the strength of our families and communities, and to the adequacy of our worldview, than we do to being involved in God's battle plan, according to which we first give ourselves and then we give more than we can afford. Maybe we think that God is "in his heaven" and there is no battle to fight. Or maybe we think it is a losing battle. Or maybe we think the turning point of history is still ahead of us. Maybe we need to be reminded, as Paul would remind us, of the victory of resurrection.

> To Christ shall all the nations bow,
> and sing with you this song;
> "Uplifted are the gates of brass,
> the bars of iron yield;
> behold the King of Glory pass;
> the cross hath won the field!"[7]

6. See Oscar Cullman, *Christ and Time* (London: SCM, 1951), 84.
7. From "Lift Up Your Heads, Ye Gates of Brass."

The Author

John Howard Yoder (1927–1997) taught ethics and theology at Notre Dame University and Associated Mennonite Biblical Seminary. He received his doctorate from the University of Basel, Switzerland, and was a member of Prairie Street Mennonite Church in Elkhart, Indiana. Widely recognized around the world as a theological educator, ethicist, and interpreter of biblical pacifism, he is best known for his seminal book *The Politics of Jesus*.

The Editors

John C. Nugent (PhD, Calvin Theological Seminary) is professor of Old Testament at Great Lakes Christian College in Lansing, Michigan. He is the author of *The Politics of Yahweh* (Cascade Books, 2011) and the editor of *The End of Sacrifice* (Herald Press, 2011) and *Radical Ecumenicity* (ACU Press, 2010). He also heads up the John Howard Yoder Indexing Project and serves as a consulting editor for the *Stone-Campbell Journal*.

Andy Alexis-Baker is currently a PhD candidate in systematic theology and theological ethics at Marquette University. In addition to publishing numerous articles in academic journals, he is the coeditor of John Howard Yoder's *Christian Attitudes to War, Peace, and Revolution* (Brazos, 2009) and *Theology of Missions* (IVP Academic, 2013). Andy is also the general coeditor of the Peaceable Kingdom Series with Cascade Books.

Branson L. Parler (PhD, Calvin Theological Seminary) is associate professor of theological studies at Kuyper College in Grand Rapids, Michigan. He is author of *Things Hold Together: John Howard Yoder's Trinitarian Theology of Culture* (Herald Press, 2012). He also participates in the John Howard Yoder Indexing Project (www.yoderindex.com).